ESSENTIAL
MENTORING
TECHNIQUES

ESSENTIAL MENTORING TECHNIQUES: MENTORING FUNDAMENTALS

We live in an age of rapid change and technological achievement. But as in ages past, the most valuable asset to any organization is still the accumulated knowledge and experience of the people who work there. So how can an organization ensure that this legacy is retained and passed on to new generations of employees? One answer is mentoring.

The word mentor comes from a character in ancient Greek mythology. In Homer's epic work The Odyssey, Mentor was a trusted advisor to Odysseus and caretaker to Odysseus's son. Athena, the goddess of wisdom, took the form of Mentor to teach and guide the boy.

In the modern business world, the objective of mentors is the same – to teach, guide, and share wisdom. When business mentoring is implemented appropriately, it can improve employees' business knowledge, foster relationships within the organization, and enhance job satisfaction and retention.

This course covers the key concepts involved in workplace mentoring. You'll discover the purpose and mutual benefits of mentoring. You'll learn about the differences between coaching and mentoring relationships. You'll find out about mentoring programs and mentoring models. You'll also learn about the characteristics that help make mentoring programs successful and about the different aspects of formal and informal mentoring.

OBJECTIVES AND BENEFITS OF MENTORING

Objectives of mentoring

In business, a mentor is someone who helps another person attain personal and professional goals that would have otherwise been achieved less effectively, more slowly, or not at all. Mentoring is the offering of guidance, advice, and information by the mentor. It's most often a one-to-one relationship between an experienced and less experienced businessperson.

At key times in a person's career, having a mentor to guide and advise can make a substantial difference to how decisions are made and how likely those choices are to have a positive result. In fact, there are few business relationships that are as beneficial and influential as that of mentor and mentee.

A well-designed mentoring program can lead to the acquisition of knowledge and expertise within a trusting and supportive environment.

The key goal of business mentoring is for the mentor to provide the mentee with career and skill development within a supportive relationship. Mentoring isn't about quick fixes for issues or about strict supervision of employees. Nor does it take the place of training. The main objectives of mentoring are to offer long-term career guidance and exploration, provide skill development, set a behavioral model for the mentee to emulate, and arrange opportunities for networking and building business relationships.

Select each objective for more information.

Offer career guidance

Mentors offer mentees valuable career guidance. They can help the mentee hone in on a suitable occupational field, encourage professional behavior, and help build professional confidence.

Provide skill development

Mentors provide mentees with advice on skill development. They are a valuable resource for determining what skills are needed for progression along the mentee's chosen career path.

Set a behavioral model

Mentees learn by observing their mentor as a behavioral model. By observing how their mentors behave, they come to an understanding of what they should do in a similar context.

Arrange opportunities for networking

Mentors arrange opportunities for networking and developing relationships. Mentors can introduce mentees to key people, recommend mentees as members of committees, and encourage their inclusion in workplace programs.

Consider this example. Dhara is a senior manager at a logistics company that specializes in transporting consumer goods. Mike is a junior manager who's been with the company for less than a year. Dhara is meeting with Mike for the first time as part of a mentoring program at the company.

Follow along as Dhara and Mike discuss their mentoring relationship.

Dhara: I'm glad to meet with you, Mike. I'm very supportive of our company's mentoring program, and I hope I'll be able to help you in your career with us.

Dhara says, pleasantly.

Mike: I'm looking forward to it. I'm particularly interested in logistical analytics and optimization. I know that's one of your areas of expertise.

Mike says, happily.

Dhara: Well, it seems we're a good match. From my experience, I can tell you that you'll need an aptitude for mathematics and statistics.

Mike: I'm good with numbers but I haven't had a lot of experience or specific training in logistics yet. I'm not really sure what I need to concentrate on.

Mike says, thoughtfully

Dhara: First of all, I'd suggest getting some training in using our company's IT and telecommunications systems. As for experience, you'll learn a lot if you work on projects that involve supply chain management.

Dhara says, pleasantly.

Mike: That sounds exciting, but I can't just do what I want. I'm just starting out in the business, after all.

Mike says, sincerely.

Dhara: I'll tell you what. I'm going to introduce you to André, our distribution manager. He's just starting a project aimed at improving the efficiency of the customer order cycle and its associated information systems. He could use a junior member on his team. Would you be interested in meeting him?

Dhara says, pleasantly.

Mike: Yeah, I would. It sounds like a great opportunity to learn the business, and get to know some new people as well.

Mike says, happily.

In her first meeting with Mike, Dhara achieved the key objectives of mentoring. She offered career guidance and provided Mike with the opportunity to develop his skills.

She also arranged an opportunity to network and build business relationships. And Dhara indicated that over time she'll act as a behavioral model that Mike can emulate when handling logistical analytics and optimization issues.

Workplace mentoring programs provide many benefits to the organization as well as to the participants. These programs are useful for achieving objectives such as effective recruitment and orientation of new hires, succession planning and knowledge transfer, professional development, and retention of talent.

Select each objective for more information on the benefits of mentoring.

Recruitment and orientation of new hires

When an organization is competing for qualified employees, a mentoring program can give it an advantage. Mentoring programs support individuals both personally and professionally. Many top candidates regard mentoring programs as a sign the organization is committed to offering opportunities and preparing them for advancement once they're hired.

Succession planning

Mentoring helps an organization transfer knowledge from experienced employees to new workers. A mentoring program can be an important part of succession planning – the process of developing internal talent to take over positions within the organization. Both mentoring and succession programs increase the capacity of the organization to develop and retain knowledge capital and ensure leadership continuity in key roles.

Professional development

As people's lives change, so do their expectations and aspirations for the future. Mentoring can help employees chart career paths and set goals for professional growth. Or it can open up new opportunities for career transitions.

Retention of talent

Mentoring can help retain talented people because employees have a stronger connection to the organization. Mentored employees are less likely to leave because they're supported in their work and they're kept informed about new opportunities within the organization.

Question

What are the key objectives of workplace mentoring?

Options:

1. To offer career guidance and exploration
2. To provide advice about skill development

3. To set a behavioral model for the mentee

4. To arrange opportunities for networking and relationship building 5. To provide quick efficient fixes for behavioral issues 6. To provide close supervision of new hires

Answer

Option 1: *This option is correct. Mentors are a valuable resource for information about the opportunities available for career advancement.*

Option 2: *This option is correct. Mentors are a good resource for discussing and determining the training or hands-on experience a mentee should pursue to achieve career goals.*

Option 3: *This option is correct. Mentors act as behavioral models to mentees, who learn from observation.*

Option 4: *This option is correct. Mentors help mentees develop personal and professional relationships.*

Option 5: *This option is incorrect. A mentoring relationship is supportive and developmental. It's not a resource for quick fixes.*

Option 6: *This option is incorrect. Mentoring is the offering of guidance, advice, and information. It's not about micromanaging.*

Benefits for mentees

Traditionally, mentoring is a partnership between two individuals, the mentee and the mentor. But in workplace mentoring there's a third partner – the organization that hosts the mentoring relationship. Effective mentoring has benefits for all three mentoring partners. And each partner must contribute to the mutually beneficial experience.

Arguably, the most obvious benefits of a mentoring relationship are to the mentee.

A productive mentoring relationship can make the difference between making career mistakes and strategically avoiding them, and between advancing quickly in an organization's hierarchy and stagnating in a dead-end job.

The mentee benefits from a mentoring relationship by receiving emotional support, feedback, career focus, and by developing an understanding of the organization's business culture.

Select each mentee benefit for more information.

emotional support

Emotional support is a key element of a productive mentoring relationship. The mentor is an emotional anchor with whom the mentee can share concerns as well as successes. Unlike simple training, mentoring offers comradeship, counseling, and sympathetic emotional acceptance.

feedback

Mentors provide mentees with critical feedback in key areas of business and career development. Mentees develop and learn through conversations with their more experienced mentors who share knowledge and skills that can be incorporated into the mentees' thinking and practice.

career focus

Mentoring helps mentees develop a sharper career focus, helping them understand what's needed to grow professionally. Effective mentors provide assistance and suggest activities which help their mentees' career progression. Mentors also help mentees understand the specific criteria for achieving rewards such as promotions and raises.

understanding business culture

Being mentored can help people understand complex organizational networks. Mentees can learn who to direct their questions to, where to go for specific professional advice, and how to maintain long-term professional relationships. Through mentoring, they'll quickly adapt to the organization's accepted behaviors and attitudes, expectations for communication and interaction, and approaches to decision making and problem solving.

Dhara has been mentoring Mike for about a year. She's meeting with him to talk about a project he's just finished. This was Mike's first time as an assistant project manager. Follow along as Dhara and Mike discuss Mike's progress.

Dhara: Mike, how are you feeling now that you've finished your first project as an assistant manager? I know you had some ups and downs, but that's to be expected.

Mike: I'm glad you said that. It helped when I could come and talk through my problems and concerns with you along the way.

Dhara: From my observation, many of the issues you had during the project stemmed from how you communicated with your team. If you can improve those skills, things will go a lot smoother next time.

Mike: Yeah. I'm so used to doing things myself. I had a problem delegating tasks to other people. Things got better after you and I talked it over, though.

Mike says, sincerely.

Dhara: In some organizations, team members work autonomously, but at our company your team will look to you for guidance. That's the way we work on a team.

Mike: I enjoyed being a leader, and we did get the project in on time and under budget. I hope I'll get to be a full project manager soon.

Mike says, pleased.

Dhara: I'm proud of you. Now tell me, have you thought about taking any of the training the company offers? There are several good communication courses.

Dhara says, sincerely.

Mike: Actually, there's a software programming course that sounds like fun.

Mike says, enthusiastically.

Dhara: Do you think you need that course to become a project manager? You've already taken the training in IT and telecommunications. What do you think would benefit your career the most?

Mike: You're right that my communication skills could use improving. Thanks for steering me back on track.

Mike says, sincerely.

Mike and Dhara's mentoring relationship has provided a number of benefits for Mike. Dhara gave him emotional support both when he succeeded and when he ran into problems.

She gave him critical feedback on his performance as an assistant project manager, and she helped him understand the business culture of the organization by talking to him about teamwork.

She also helped him focus on his career by steering him toward the training he needed to be an effective project manager.

Jenny is a new employee in the Human Resources Department of a large university. Although Jenny was hired as a junior administrative assistant, she hopes to move into a career in educational counseling. To further her plans, Jenny has applied and been accepted to the university's mentoring program.

Question

What will be the benefits of mentoring for Jenny as a mentee?

Options:

1. Emotional support will be a part of the mentoring relationship
2. Her mentor will provide her with constructive feedback
3. She'll understand the organization's business culture
4. She'll have a sharper career focus
5. She'll be promoted rapidly
6. She'll earn more money than unmentored colleagues

Answer

Option 1: This option is correct. Jenny's mentor will offer her comradeship, counseling, and sympathetic emotional acceptance.

Option 2: This option is correct. A mentor will provide Jenny with critical feedback in key areas of business and career development.

Option 3: This option is correct. Being mentored can help Jenny understand the organization's accepted procedures, behaviors, and perspectives.

Option 4: This option is correct. Jenny's mentor can help her understand the criteria that will help her focus on her career.

Option 5: This option is incorrect. Mentoring will be useful for sharpening Jenny's career focus, but it can't guarantee rewards such as promotion.

Option 6: This option is incorrect. Mentoring can help a mentee focus on career objectives such as salary level, but Jenny's objective isn't financial.

Benefits to mentors

It's clear that mentees benefit from the mentoring relationship, but mentors benefit as well. Benefits to mentors include professional growth, personal satisfaction, and enhanced understanding of the organization and how it works.

See each mentor benefit for more information.

Professional growth

For mentors, mentoring can be an opportunity for professional growth. Mentors not only teach their mentees but learn from them as well. Mentees can be a source of fresh ideas, insights, and new social and professional contacts. And working with mentees helps mentors develop their own leadership and communication skills. This in turn can enhance their own career prospects.

Personal satisfaction

Mentors gain great personal satisfaction and pride from contributing to mentees' growth and development. Some also find it satisfying to know that their expert knowledge and experience is being handed to someone else and will continue to benefit the organization.

Enhanced understanding of the organization

Mentoring allows mentors to work with people of different cultures, generations, backgrounds, values, and levels of expertise. Mentors often gain new perspectives and knowledge when mentees question why things are done a certain way. This can stimulate a fresh look at how work processes can be improved.

Mike has now been working at the logistics company for two years. He's meeting with his mentor, Dhara, for a mentoring session. Mike has recently finished working as a project manager on a major initiative that involved a lot of traveling.

Dhara: So, Mike, we haven't met in a while, but I've enjoyed your e-mails. You seem to have done well with your first project as manager.

Mike: It was great. As you know, we developed an analytics program to identify trends in our supply chain infrastructure. It really gave me confidence to know I could e-mail you for advice, even though we couldn't always meet in person.

Dhara: I'm really pleased with your progress and how you've grown as a manager. So how did you finally make out with analyzing the warehousing data?

Dhara is proud.

Mike: Well, I appreciated your suggestions, but actually I came up with my own idea. It balances outbound and inbound goods with improved efficiency. I can show you later, if you'd like.

Mike says, sincerely.

Dhara: Sure, I'd like that. *Dhara says, interested.*

Mike: Great. Maybe we can do that this afternoon. I'm meeting with Mr. Anderson from the head office to demonstrate the program. He's one of the new vice presidents. Would you like to join us?

Mike says, pleased.

Dhara: I'd love to meet him. *Dhara says, pleased.*

Mike: Great. I'll see you at two o'clock in the boardroom. *Mike says, enthusiastic.*

Mentoring Mike provided a number of benefits for Dhara, including great personal satisfaction from seeing him succeed.

She also got the opportunity to enhance her understanding of the organization by learning about Mike's new approach to analyzing warehousing data.

And through her contact with Mike, Dhara gained the opportunity to meet an important business contact and enhance her own professional growth.

Remember Jenny, the new employee at a university? She's been accepted into the organization's mentoring program. Jenny has decided that Omar, the chief administrator of the university's Department of Admissions, would be a productive mentor for her. Omar has agreed to act as mentor and the two have met to discuss the mentoring relationship.

Question
What will be the benefits of mentoring for Omar as a mentor?
Options:
1. Omar will gain personal satisfaction from seeing Jenny succeed and passing on his administrative knowledge
2. He'll gain an enhanced understanding of the organizational culture of the university
3. He'll enhance his own professional growth
4. Omar will be able to delegate some of his work to Jenny
5. Omar can transfer Jenny to his department once she's gained the necessary skills

Answer
Option 1: *This option is correct. Mentors gain personal satisfaction from contributing to their mentees' development and by passing expert knowledge on to their mentees.*
Option 2: *This option is correct. Mentors often gain new perspectives and knowledge by working with mentees.*
Option 3: *This option is correct. Mentees can be a valuable source of fresh ideas, insights, and new social and professional contacts.*
Option 4: *This option is incorrect. The purpose of mentoring is to pass on knowledge and encourage emotional growth. It's not to take over the mentor's workload.*
Option 5: *This option is incorrect. Mentoring is about the mentee's desired career path, not the mentor's wishes.*

4. Benefits to organizations
Mentoring is beneficial to all parties involved in its practice: mentees, mentors and the organizations for which they work. Benefits to the organization include improved interorganizational communication, a better retention rate than organizations without a mentoring program, and increased employee support for the organization's strategic business initiatives.

See each benefit for more information.

Improved communication
A mentoring program is beneficial to building communication capabilities within an organization. Mentoring provides an avenue for employees to find resources and answers to questions. It enables them to understand more quickly how to do their jobs and what their responsibilities are. Mentoring also reduces the loss of tacit knowledge as senior employees retire from the workforce.

Better retention rate
Mentoring relationships can help retain talented people because they have a commitment to their mentors and, by extension, to the organization. Employees are less likely to "job hop" if they feel supported in their work and made aware of opportunities by their mentors.

Support for strategic initiatives
Mentoring programs help mentees understand an organization's business strategy and how individual efforts support corporate goals. When businesses fail to align employee knowledge with strategy, significant time and effort may be expended on initiatives that have minimal impact, while key issues or opportunities are overlooked.

Mentoring programs are most beneficial when linked to the organization's strategic goals.
For example, a company forecasting growth could use a mentoring program to prepare promising employees for future managerial positions.
Or consider an organization facing a high retirement rate. That company could benefit from a mentoring program to help facilitate continuity of departing employees' technical skills and organizational knowledge.
Jenny is a mentee in the mentoring program of a large university. Her mentor is Omar, the chief administrator of the Department of Admissions. Jenny wants to work in educational coun-

seling, and Omar is working with her to develop a career path at the university.

Question
What are the benefits of mentoring for the university as the supporting organization?
Options:
1. The communication within the university's business hierarchy will be improved
2. The university will have a better employee retention rate than organizations without a mentoring program
3. Jenny will be more supportive of the university's strategic business initiatives
4. The university will be able to reduce the cost of training employees and upgrading skills
5. The university will see an immediate improvement in Jenny's job performance Answer
Option 1: This option is correct. Mentoring programs provide an avenue for employees to find resources and answers to questions about their jobs and responsibilities.
Option 2: This option is correct. Jenny will be more likely to stay at the university because she feels supported and because her mentor made her aware of opportunities.
Option 3: This option is correct. Mentoring programs help mentees understand an organization's business strategy, and how their individual efforts support corporate goals and initiatives.
Option 4: This option is incorrect. Mentoring programs enhance knowledge and skills but don't replace the need for training and professional development.
Option 5: This option is incorrect. Jenny's performance may be enhanced by mentoring, but the point of the program is to help her manage her long-term career objectives.

Summary
The main objectives of workplace mentoring are career guidance and exploration, skill development, setting behavioral

models, and arranging opportunities for networking and building business relationships.

Effective mentoring benefits all three mentoring partners – mentee, mentor, and organization. Mentee benefits include emotional support, feedback, career focus, and developing an understanding of the organization's business culture. Mentor benefits include professional development, personal satisfaction, and enhanced understanding of how the organization works. Organization benefits include improved communication between employees, a better retention rate than organizations without a mentoring program, and increased employee support for the organization's strategic business initiatives.

MENTORING, COACHING, AND MANAGING

Mentoring and coaching

Mentoring is what is known as a "developmental relationship." These types of relationships involve an experienced business-person taking an active interest in a colleague and actively helping to improve that person's potential. In business, the two most common types of developmental relationships are mentoring and coaching.

Coaching and mentoring are alike in many ways and have some purposes in common. Both types of relationships are used to nurture employees' skills and achieve business objectives.

Both approaches are used to challenge and help individuals change the way they work, identify and solve problems, make decisions, overcome obstacles, and implement change.

Coaching and mentoring sessions are also similar in that each involves a series of meetings or encounters that make use of focused discussions about goals and objectives. Between sessions, the individual practices new techniques, approaches, and working styles. In later meetings, the individual's experiences may be discussed and any arising issues or consequences are analyzed.

Reflect

What do you think are the general differences between coaching and mentoring?

The differences between coaching and mentoring.

As you may have noted, coaching involves a directive style of development, while mentoring involves an enabling style. In general, coaches focus on more practical, goal-focused objectives. It's usually a short-term intervention, or series of interventions, intended to develop specific results by a particular point in time. In contrast, mentors encourage a committed, long-term relationship in which the mentor supports the emotional growth and professional business development of a mentee.

Coaching is a good approach to dealing with task-oriented, skills-focused, and time-sensitive issues. It's equally effective for helping individuals achieve results and improve performance either individually or as part of a team.

Mentoring involves some aspects of coaching, but it's more than that. At its heart, mentoring is more about developing the person than simply improving performance. Mentoring gives an individual the ability to apply skills, knowledge, and experience to new situations. The fundamental differences between the two types of relationships involve the areas of focus, function, relationship, authority, reward, and area of activity.

See each area for more information on the differences between coaching and mentoring.

Focus

The focus of coaching is on a specific agenda with measurable outcomes. It's mainly concerned with developing skills and strategies to achieve shorter-term performance objectives. In coaching, the goal or objective is often predetermined, as is the coach's plan for achieving it.

In contrast, mentoring focuses on personal growth and the continuous improvement of an individual's capability and potential. Together the mentor and mentee develop an ongoing process that helps the mentee grow and mature as a businessperson.

Function

The function, or purpose, of coaching is to help an individual achieve specific objectives. In many cases, these objectives are established before the coaching begins. Coaches often solve issues by offering advice or prescribing a recommended approach.

The function of mentoring is to develop mentees to a point where they can make mature and intelligent career decisions for themselves. Unlike coaches, mentors facilitate and teach, allowing mentees to discover their own direction. Mentors often approach issues by using questioning processes that force the mentees to discover solutions for themselves.

Relationship

In a coaching relationship, the coachee is usually assigned to the coach, who assumes the responsibility for improving performance. When an issue arises, it's usually the coach who suggests a solution. The agreed-upon schedule for achieving objectives is often prioritized over personal issues.

In mentoring, the mentee often chooses the mentor. In turn, the mentor creates a safe environment where the mentee is able to talk freely and confidentially. Mentors deal with issues by encouraging and guiding mentees to form their own solutions on their own time. Solutions to issues are adapted to the particular situation, and mentors' advice is intended to stimulate personal reflection, analytical thinking, and discussion.

Authority

In a coaching relationship, the coach is generally in authority and is in charge of managing the objectives to be achieved, and the method of achieving them. Coaches use structured and focused instruction and have the right to expect a degree of compliance from coachees.

Ideally, mentoring involves a power-free relationship based on mutual acceptance. A mentor's influence is proportionate to the value provided to the mentee. Even if the mentor is more highly ranked within the organization's business hierarchy, that authority is tempered within the mentoring relationship.

Reward

A coach's rewards are usually the form of value from the coachee's improved job performance. Coaches don't usually expect to learn from their coachees.

Mentoring is a more reciprocal relationship. Both the mentor and the mentee learn from each other and grow professionally. Mentors benefit from an enhanced reputation when their mentees succeed in business. Also, mentors often discover new ways of doing things from mentees and may gain a revitalized interest in their own work.

Area of activity

Organizations use coaching when employees need help to achieve specific objectives or perform given tasks. The coach is generally work oriented and focuses primarily on short- term objectives involving the coachee's job performance.

Organizations use mentoring for broader purposes, such as developing managerial talent, or succession planning. Mentors don't direct mentees, but rather they provide opportunities for them by showing them how to operate within an organization's business hierarchy, or helping them network with important business contacts.

Question

Match the type of developmental relationship to its characteristics. Each type will match to more than one characteristic.

Options:

A. Coaching

B. Mentoring

Targets:

1. The focus is on shorter-term work performance objectives

2. The function is to advise an individual on how to achieve particular goals

3. The relationship encourages reaching decisions through personal reflection, analytical thinking, and discussion

4. Neither party in the relationship has strict authority over the other

5. Rewards are usually the form of value from improved job performance
6. Areas of activity include an organization's development of managerial talent, or succession planning

Answer

The focus of coaching is on work performance objectives, while mentoring is more about personal and professional growth.

The function of coaching is to help an individual achieve particular goals. The function of mentoring is to develop an individual's capacity to make intelligent decisions.

In a mentoring relationship, a mentor's advice is intended to stimulate reflection, analytical thinking, and discussion. In a coaching relationship, it's usually the coach who prescribes a solution or course of action for the coachee.

Mentoring involves a power-free relationship based on mutual acceptance. In coaching, the coach is generally in authority and expects compliance from the coachee.

A coach's rewards are usually the form of the coachee's improved job performance. In mentoring, both the mentor and mentee grow professionally.

Mentoring involves longer-term areas of activity such as developing employees to succeed into senior roles in the business hierarchy.

Coaching and mentoring in action

Consider this example. Mathemetric Manufacturing Group is a multinational company. The organization makes use of both coaching and mentoring to aid in the professional development of its employees.

However, the company's approaches to the two programs differ in ways typical of both coaching and mentoring. Shey and Tori are involved in the company's coaching program. Shey is a senior marketing manager, and Tori is a junior sales representative.

Join Shey and Tori as they participate in a coaching session.

Shey: Okay, Tori, you mentioned you were concerned because you didn't meet your sales quota last month. Let's focus on that.

Shey is helpful.

Tori: I thought I had reached my sales quota, but two customers backed out at the last minute. I guess they just got cold feet. *Tori is puzzled.*

Shey: Well, your goal for next month is to meet your targets.

Tori: What do you think I should do differently?

Tori is puzzled.

Shey: Here's what I'd do. Keep in close contact with the customers. Get those contracts to them quickly and don't give their enthusiasm a chance to cool. If you leave customers on their own too long, they're bound to start second guessing their decisions. Got that?

Tori: Right. Keep in contact and get those contracts signed. *Tori is sincere.*

Shey: Okay. I'm expecting you to meet your sales goals next month. Don't disappoint me.

Tori: No, sir! *Tori is happy.*

Shey and Tori's developmental relationship is typical of coaching in six areas: focus, function, relationship, authority, reward, and area of activity.

See each area for more information.

Focus

The focus of coaching is short term and work-related. In their coaching session, Shey and Tori were working on a short-term performance objective.

Function

The function, or purpose, of coaching is to help an individual achieve specific objectives. As is typical of coaching, Shey prescribed an approach to Tori's issue.

Relationship

In coaching, it's the coach who assumes the responsibility for improving performance. Here, Shey prioritized the schedule for achieving Tori's sales objective and gave her instructional advice on how to achieve it.

Authority

The authority in a coaching relationship lies mainly with the coach. In this relationship, Shey was in control and was comfortable telling Tori what to do.

Reward

If his coaching is successful, Shey's reward will be Tori's improved job performance.

Area of activity

The area of activity is typical of coaching because the issue and Shey's prescribed solution concern a specific short-term business objective.

Eloise and Jason also work for Mathemetric Manufacturing Group. They're involved in the company's mentoring program. Eloise is the director of communications. She mentors Jason, one of the company's public relations officers.

Follow along as Eloise and Jason participate in a mentoring session.

Eloise: So, Jason, I hear you ran into a bit of an issue dealing with a local news reporter. Is this something you'd like to talk about?

Eloise is pleasant.

Jason: That was a mess. The guy said he was interested in our new manufacturing plant. Then when we met, he started asking me all these questions about some product recall I didn't even know about.

Jason is concerned.

Eloise: Handling media relations is an important ability when you work in PR. It takes time and effort to develop those skills. And that won't be the last ambush interview you'll be involved in.

Jason: I tried to be professional and answer the questions, but I didn't have any information. Then the reporter wrote a bunch of stuff in his article that I didn't even say. Well...don't think I said them, anyway.

Eloise: What do you think would have helped you avoid that situation?

Jason: I guess I need to know how to communicate to the media

– how to regain control when I'm blindsided – and how to make sure I'm not misquoted.

Jason is sincere.

Eloise: When I first started working, I used to attend the Public Relations Association's annual convention. They often have workshops on media relations, and it's also an opportunity to network with seasoned professionals. Does that sound interesting to you?

Jason: Yeah. Attending the conference could be really valuable to me. How long has it been since you've been to the event?

Eloise: Oh, it's been a number of years. I've been so busy. But you know, you've made me think that attending is something I should do as well. Maybe I'll learn a few new things as well. *Eloise is happy.*

Eloise and Jason's relationship is typical of mentoring in the same six areas as Eloise and Jason's relationship is typical of coaching. These are focus, function, relationship, authority, reward, and area of activity.

See each area for more information.

Focus

The mentoring relationship focuses on improvement of the mentee's capability and potential. Eloise and Jason's session focused on Jason's professional growth.

Function

The function of mentoring is to develop mentees' ability to make mature and intelligent decisions for themselves. In this relationship, Eloise encouraged Jason to make his own decisions.

Relationship

The relationship between a mentor and mentee should stimulate personal reflection. Eloise didn't dictate a solution; she used a questioning process to guide Jason to a solution through self-examination.

Authority

Mentoring doesn't involve an imbalance in authority. Mentor

and mentee are partners in a relationship based on mutual acceptance. In this relationship, mentor Eloise offered guidance but didn't dictate any action to Jason.

Reward

One of the rewards for mentors is professional growth and renewed interest in work. Through her mentoring, Eloise realized that she could grow professionally if she started attending the conference again.

Area of activity

The area of activity encompassed by mentoring is wide ranging and long term. Eloise's

mentoring of Jason involved helping him network and providing him with opportunities to improve his career prospects.

Mentoring and management

Managers often have excellent coaching and mentoring skills. The primary responsibility of managers is to achieve specific organizational goals through their direct reports. Because of this, managers can be effective coaches to employees under their direct control.

Because coaching is results oriented, managers may act as coaches for their direct reports – setting goals and establishing performance plans.

But mentoring is different in that it's most often a voluntary relationship that succeeds best with a balance of power.

Even in formal mentoring programs, mentors are rarely direct supervisors of their mentees. This encourages mentees to develop independence and self-reliance.

Managing and mentoring both have important roles to play in terms of developing skilled and competent employees. Both roles involve creating value, guiding behavior, and creating opportunities for employees to succeed professionally. But there are differences.

A mentoring relationship focuses on developing the mentee both professionally and personally.

Unlike managers, mentors don't evaluate the mentee with respect to job performance. They don't conduct performance reviews of the mentee or hold control over rewards such as salary increases and promotions.

This is so mentors can provide a safe learning environment. Mentees can discuss issues openly and honestly without worrying about negative consequences.

Question
Callinsure Insurance is a large insurance company with an extensive employee developmental program that includes both coaching and mentoring.

More than one option may match to each relationship.

Options:
A. Priya and Gideon
B. Ross and Shanisse
C. Mai and Tony
D. Rajit and Deborah

Targets:
1. Coaching 2. Mentoring
Answer

Priya and Gideon's developmental relationship is typical of coaching. Gideon was assigned to be in the relationship with Priya. Also, the focus is on developing skills to achieve shorter-term performance objectives.

Ross and Shanisse are also typical of coaching in that the function is for the coach to prescribe a recommended approach.

Mai and Tony's developmental relationship is typical of mentoring in that Tony chose Mai as his mentor, and Mai didn't hold any authority over him within the relationship.

Rajit and Deborah also have a mentoring relationship as the main area of activity was personal development of Deborah's ability to manage people.

Understanding mentoring
It's important to be able to understand the differences between mentoring and coaching. This will help you recognize the im-

portance of the personal aspect of mentoring relationships. This allows the mentor to go beyond teaching short-term goals and help the mentee with developing confidence, self- awareness, and a healthy work-life balance.

Understanding mentoring will also help you understand that it's an ongoing capacity-building process.

The purpose of mentoring is to develop an individual to handle the future, not just the immediate job or task that needs doing.

And perhaps most important, when you truly understand mentoring, you'll be better prepared to take on a mentoring role and pass on your skills and knowledge to a new generation.

Question

Why is it important to be able to distinguish between the mentoring and coaching roles?

Options:

1. You'll recognize the importance of the personal element in mentoring relationships
2. You'll understand that mentoring develops the individual for the future, not just for a specific job or task
3. You'll be better prepared to take on a mentoring role
4. You'll be better able to mentor people you manage
5. You'll be able to make sure employees meet all short-term and long-term performance goals

Answer

Option 1: *This option is correct. Mentoring involves personal elements such as self- confidence, self-awareness, and work-life balance.*

Option 2: *This option is correct. Mentoring is an ongoing capacity-building process.*

Option 3: *This option is correct. You need to truly understand mentoring in order to pass on*
your skills and knowledge.

Option 4: *This option is incorrect. Mentoring relationships work best as a voluntary relationship when there's a balance of power.*

Option 5: *This option is incorrect. You can't guarantee all goals will be met. But mentoring can impart skills and competencies individ-*

uals need to develop.

Summary

Mentoring and coaching are types of developmental relationships. Coaching involves a directive style of development, while mentoring involves an enabling style. Coaches focus on practical, goal-focused objectives. In contrast, mentors encourage a committed, long-term relationship supporting the emotional growth and professional development of a mentee. The fundamental differences between the two types of relationships involve the areas of focus, function, influence, reward, and area of activity.

Understanding mentoring will help you recognize the importance of mentoring's personal element, understand that mentoring develops the individual for the future, and prepare you to take on a mentoring role of your own.

MENTORING MODELS AND APPROACHES

Successful mentoring programs

Poorly-planned mentoring can be a waste of time. Mentoring relationships can fail for a number of reasons including lack of interest, poor participation, unrealistic expectations, and a failure to align mentoring with an organization's strategic objectives. Many organizations have chosen to support and protect mentoring relationships by establishing mentoring programs. These programs formalize the expectations each partner has for the relationship and ensure the interests of the organization are aligned with those of mentors and mentees.

Successful business mentoring programs are individually suited to the particular circumstances of each organization and its employees. But effective mentoring programs also share characteristics that are essential for success. Successful programs need support from the organization's leaders, effective coordination of the program, trained mentors and well-matched participants, ongoing support, and effective assessment of the program.

The first characteristic of successful mentoring programs is **support from leaders**. Senior business leaders are decision makers. They have the power to allocate funding, champion the program, and participate in the program as mentors.

Successful mentoring initiatives require visible and consistent support from an organization's business leaders. Their support is imperative for building a culture of mentorship within the organization.

The organization will also benefit from leaders' support of mentoring. As partners in the mentoring program, leaders can ensure that mentees are developed in alignment with the organization's business objectives.

The second characteristic of successful mentoring programs is **effective coordination.** It includes marketing the program to employees and providing support for selecting and recruiting participants. Most successful mentoring programs have someone dedicated to managing and administering the mentoring program. This coordinator has the responsibility of ensuring the program is both relevant and flexible enough to meet the changing needs and requirements of the mentoring partners.

See each aspect of effective coordination for more information.

Marketing to employees

Communication is crucial in ensuring a successful mentoring program. Marketing the program to employees will effectively publicize the benefits and results of the program. It will also help recruit mentors and mentees.

Selection and recruitment

A well-coordinated program can help with careful selection and recruitment of mentoring partners. Coordination can ensure that partners are well matched, and that diversity is respected. It can also make sure that no willing employee is left out of the program.

The third characteristic of successful mentoring programs is **trained mentors and matched participants**. Well organized mentoring programs encompass both mentor training and effective matching to ensure a productive and positive mentoring experience.

Training is essential for mentors. Even employees with years of experience may not intuitively know how to mentor another person. A training program will make sure participants have the communication skills, self-confidence, and foundational knowledge to become good mentors.

An effective method of matching mentors and mentees is also important. Leaving participants to rely on their own networks and resources to find each other can result in mismatches, or in employees being left out of the program.

The fourth characteristic of a successful mentoring program is **ongoing support** for the program. Organizations with effective programs support both mentors and mentees. Participants are allowed time for regular meetings and interactions, and mentoring responsibilities are acknowledged as part of the development of employees. This support ensures the mentoring program is perceived as credible and valued by the organization, which in turn stimulates recruitment.

The fifth characteristic of a successful mentoring program is **effective assessment** of the program. Assessment is an indispensable step in ensuring the continuity of a successful mentoring program.

Evaluation of the program will provide important data and feedback about the successes of the program, its value to the organization, and the areas that need be developed to ensure improvement.

Mentors, mentees, and the organization all participate in assessing a successful mentoring program. Mentors assess the effectiveness of the match, and whether they have the support and resources to develop the mentee.

Mentees assess whether the program is helping them achieve their developmental objectives.

Organizations assess the program through its return on investment – the cost of the program versus the value produced in the form of retention and development of employees.

Question
What are the characteristics of successful mentoring programs?
Options:
1. Support from leaders
2. Coordination and marketing of the program
3. Trained mentors and matched participants

4. Ongoing support for the program

5. Program assessment

6. A large, formal structure

7. Allowing mentors and mentees to find each other

Answer

Option 1: *This option is correct. Support from business leaders gives credibility to the program and ensures it's developed in alignment with the organization's business objectives.*

Option 2: *This option is correct. Effective coordination includes marketing the program to employees and facilitating careful selection and recruitment of mentoring partners.*

Option 3: *This option is correct. Training mentors and effectively matching participants helps ensure the program meets the needs and requirements of all the mentoring partners.*

Option 4: *This option is correct. Ongoing support for the program shows that the program is valued by the organization, which in turn stimulates recruitment.*

Option 5: *This option is correct. Effective assessment allows for continuous improvement of the program.*

Option 6: *This option is incorrect. Mentoring programs are individually suited to the particular circumstances of each organization and its employees.*

Option 7: *This option is incorrect. Mentoring programs should be proactive in matching the right mentors and mentees. This ensures people aren't left out of the program.*

Types of mentoring

Each mentor and each mentee is different, and these differences are what make each mentoring relationship unique. Although successful mentoring programs share certain characteristics, each mentoring relationship is unique and you can choose from a number of different types of mentoring.

Models and types of mentoring include one-to-one mentoring, group or team mentoring, executive mentoring, and e-mentoring.

See each model or type of mentoring for a definition.

One-to-one mentoring
One-to-one mentoring involves a relationship between two individuals – the mentor and the mentee.

Group or team mentoring
Group or team mentoring is a one-to-many type of mentoring. Either a mentor acts as a learning leader to a group of mentees, or a mentee accesses a group of mentors. Participants may be from the same work unit or may be a cross-functional group.

Executive mentoring
Executive mentoring is a mentoring relationship where a professional mentor works with a top-level executive.

E-mentoring
E-mentoring is a mentoring relationship conducted primarily through the use of electronic communication. Technology may include e-mail, online discussion groups, video conferencing, instant messaging, and phone conversations as the medium for interaction.

One-to-one mentoring is the most traditional and most common model of mentoring. It involves two people working together to develop the personal and professional skills of the mentee.

Many employees prefer this style because it enables both mentor and mentee to develop a closer, more personal relationship. It also provides individual support and attention for the mentee.

This type of relationship is particularly beneficial for the performance and career progression of an employee within an organization. However, it can be resource intensive for the organization to track the many pairings in a mentoring program. Also, the mentee has only the benefit of one person's viewpoint and opinions.

Group or team mentoring is often a more practical and wider ranging approach to mentoring. The mentor-to-mentees model can be useful when there are a few mentors that are highly sought after, or when mentees can benefit from interacting with both a mentor and peers.

The mentors-to-mentee approach is beneficial because a mentee can choose from numerous mentors, each with specialized knowledge. Mentees may also seek out multiple mentors to get different viewpoints on a subject of inquiry.

But despite its benefits, group mentoring doesn't offer the same level of intimacy, privacy, and personal attention as one-to-one mentoring.

Question

Match the type of mentoring to the definition. Each type may match to more than one definition.

Options:

A. One-to-one

B. Group or team

Targets:

1. A relationship between two individuals – the mentor and the mentee
2. An experienced individual mentors a number of mentees
3. A mentee accesses several different mentors to get different viewpoints and opinions

Answer

A one to-one relationship has one mentor and one mentee.

Group or team mentoring is one-to-many, and it includes a mentor with a number of mentees.

Group or team mentoring is one-to-many, and it includes a group of mentors working with a single mentee.

Mentoring isn't just for people beginning a career. Even top-level executives benefit from working with a mentor. **Executive mentoring** is a growing field, involving professional mentors who support mentees in the higher ranks of an organization. In this type of mentoring, the mentor and mentee are often equal in business stature and the mentor is from outside the organization. Executive mentoring gives the mentee freedom to discuss and deliberate in a confidential environment, with no topic limited by company politics, or by professional relationships.

Some people are skeptical of mentoring at a distance. But the popularity of distance learning and proliferation of remote teams has contributed to a new type of mentoring known as **e-mentoring** or virtual mentoring.

An e-mentoring relationship is often a good alternative to consider when geographic distances are an issue, or when a mentee is seeking a particular mentor with specialized knowledge. E-mentoring relationships may use the one-to-one or group model of mentoring.

When an organization uses e-mentoring, it should make sure participants are computer literate and have access to computers. Participants should be offered training on how to communicate effectively using electronic media.

Inter-Swift Aeronautics is an international aeronautics company that specializes in the design and production of commercial aircraft. The company uses a number of types and models of mentoring including one-to-one mentoring, group mentoring, executive mentoring, and e-mentoring.

See each model or type of mentoring for an example of mentoring at Inter-Swift Aeronautics.

One-to-one mentoring

Aziz and Linda meet weekly and have developed a close, personal mentoring relationship. Aziz is a senior designer. And although Linda doesn't work in his department, she is interested in developing a career path that encompasses that field of endeavor.

Group or team mentoring

Khaled is a senior project manager who mentors four employees who have recently joined the company. He meets with each mentee separately and as a group in order to strengthen team-building skills.

Executive mentoring

Leyla is the chief executive officer of the company. Jean-Paul is a professional mentor from outside the organization. He works with Leyla to help her focus on the company's mission and vision, as well as to strengthen her leadership skills.

E-mentoring

Sarah and Min have a long distance mentoring relationship. Although they both work in the company's Sales Division, they're located in separate countries with different time zones. Sarah mentors Min through e-mail but also uses telephone and instant messenger to communicate during the brief period when their work hours coincide.

Types and models of mentoring are not necessarily mutually exclusive. For example, executive mentoring could use a one-to-one or a group mentoring style.

But despite the different styles, models, and types of mentoring, all mentoring relationships have characteristics in common.

They involve mentors who have the ability to help individuals in need of guidance, knowledge, and skills, and they have mentees who are looking for this help to change the direction of their lives and careers.

Question

Red Rock Publishing is a national magazine publisher. The company has a well-established mentoring program that encompasses different models and types of mentoring.

Match the type or model of mentoring to the appropriate example.

Options:

A. One-to-one mentoring

B. Group or team mentoring C. Executive mentoring

D. E-mentoring

Targets:

1. Editor Jennifer mentors copywriter Paulo. They regularly meet face to face to discuss Paulo's career object-

ives.

2. Bud is an experienced graphic artist. He mentors several employees from different functional departments at the company.

3. Indira is a professional mentor. She meets with Susan, the editor-in-chief of the company. Susan relies on Indira to provide a confidential, supportive relationship.

4. Ollie and Khan work in different regional offices of the company. Ollie mentors Khan mainly through e-mail and telephone.

Answer

One-to-one mentoring is characterized by a close relationship between two people. The main purpose is to develop the personal and professional skills of the mentee.

Group or team mentoring is a one-to-many type of mentoring. Either a mentor acts as a learning leader to a group of mentees, or a mentee accesses a group of mentors.

Executive mentoring is a type of mentoring involving professional mentors and top-level executives.

E-mentoring is a mentoring relationship conducted primarily through the use of electronic communication.

Mentoring relationships

Far from being a new phenomenon, mentoring relationships have been around for centuries. In the Middle Ages, highly-skilled craftspeople would seek the approval of their guilds to take on an apprentice. The younger worker would learn not only technical skills, but also the social and political considerations of the profession.

In the modern business world, most organizations encompass mentoring relationships. These can range all the way from the traditional informal spontaneous pairings, through to highly-structured formal relationships. But although each organization's mentoring initiative may be different, the basic idea is the same. Mentors make themselves available to mentees for consultation, conversation, and guidance.

There are many similarities between informal and formal mentoring relationships, and some relationships contain aspects of both. However, there are some basic distinctions between formal and informal mentoring.

See each style of mentoring for more information.

Formal mentoring

In formal mentoring, relationships are assigned, maintained, and monitored by the organization, usually through a highly-structured program.

The relationship adheres to an agreed-upon and documented time line, action plan, method of communication, and standard of behavior.

The programs are directly connected to an organization's strategic business objectives. And formal programs give organizations much greater control over results.

Informal mentoring

In informal mentoring, relationships don't necessarily have a structure beyond what the

mentor and mentee agree on in terms of when to meet and what to talk about.

The relationships are more "ad hoc." They change and develop, and they usually last – as long as the participants still have the time and enjoy each other's company.

The organization's input may be little more than an acknowledgment or sanction of mentoring relationships. Objectives are unspecified or arise spontaneously during the relationship and are usually confined to the mentee's personal and professional aspirations.

Reflect

Do you think formal or informal mentoring is the most common type of mentoring relationship?

You may have correctly noted that informal mentoring relationships are the most common type of mentoring relationships in the workplace. Informal relationships often spring from contact in the workplace and develop as people get to know each other. The participants may not even think of what they're doing as mentoring.

Formal and informal programs

Organizations planning mentoring programs have to consider whether to use formal or informal mentoring, or to incorporate aspects of each style. Each has its advantages and disadvantages. Informal mentoring has many benefits. There are often strong elements of friendship and empathy in an informal bond. Mentors can communicate more openly and honestly because the relationship is unrestricted by organizational interests.

Although informal mentoring can be valuable, it doesn't always work to the advantage of everyone in the workplace. Informal alliances can be exclusionary because they're often formed between people of the same gender, culture, or social position.

And while informal alliances often create a strong bond of trust between the mentor and mentee, the interests of the employer may not always be represented.

One of the major advantages of formal mentoring is that it ensures mentorship is extended to individuals who may be at a disadvantage in an informal program.

For example, a junior employee may be reluctant to ask for mentoring from someone more highly placed in the organization.

Knowing that the organization has formally approved, mentoring can empower mentees to make more advantageous matches.

The best mentoring programs combine aspects of both formal and informal mentoring. A formal structure is essential because it provides support for the organization's business objectives and provides equal access for employees.

Formal programs allow the organization more control over mentoring. Evaluating potential mentees in advance can save time, avoid mismatches, and make sure business objectives are incorporated.

But mentoring partners will create deeper and more meaningful bonds when they're allowed to operate informally within the relationship. When the mentor and mentee share a bond, they communicate more effectively and are more likely to stay in the relationship.

The optimal mentoring program for any organization will depend on its business goals, the time and resources it has to invest, and the needs of mentees.

For example, a small innovative company might use a more informal mentoring style to encourage employees to bond together within its unique business culture.

A large, conservative corporation might benefit from a much more formal mentoring style to support its long-term succession planning.

But whatever the degree of formality a mentoring program encompasses, the most important thing is that it's supported by the organization.

Relationships formed through poorly-planned and poorly-implemented programs don't provide value and won't last long. Once lost, it may be difficult to get people back into another mentoring relationship.

But well-planned programs that incorporate both formal and informal aspects of mentoring will flourish and continue to provide value to all participants involved.

Question

Categorize the style of mentoring to the arguments for implementing that style in a mentoring program. Styles may match to more than one answer.

Options:

A. Formal B. Informal

Targets:

1. The organization will have greater control over the mentoring program

2. The purpose of the relationships within the program will be

set out clearly

3. The structure of the program ensures the organization provides the resources to support the programs and the relationships therein

4. Relationships encompass a stronger degree of trust and may be more effective in achieving mentees' personal objectives

5. The mentor communicates more effectively

6. Social exclusion may be an issue

Answer

Formal mentoring is carefully planned and gives an organization more control over the program's objectives.

A formal mentoring program sets forth the main purpose of mentoring before relationships are formed.

The support of the organization and its expectations are clearly laid out in a formal mentoring program.

The trust formed through informal mentoring contributes to relationships that are closer and longer lasting than formal pairings.

Participants in informal relationships often form strong emotional bonds. This allows the mentor to communicate more effectively and honestly with the mentee.

Informal pairings are spontaneous and are often formed between people of the same gender, culture, or social position. This can reinforce social exclusion.

Summary

Successful mentoring programs need support from the organization's leaders, effective coordination of the program, trained mentors and well-matched participants, ongoing support, and effective assessment of the program.

Types and models of mentoring include one-to-one mentoring, group or team mentoring, executive mentoring, and e-mentoring.

Mentoring programs encompass different degrees of formality. Relationships range along a continuum from spontaneously-formed informal pairings through to highly-structured formal relationships.

Each type of mentoring has its benefits. Informal mentoring can create a strong emotional bond and encourages open and honest communication. Formal mentoring ensures potential mentees aren't excluded from the program and protects the interests of the employer as a partner in the relationship. The most successful programs combine elements of both formal and informal mentoring.

ESSENTIAL MENTORING TECHNIQUES: DESIGNING AND INITIATING MENTORING PROGRAMS

Mentoring is an effective way to improve performance in your organization. It enables you to link experienced individuals with less experienced colleagues. Mentors can share their knowledge and expertise with their mentees, and develop long-term working relationships with them.

In order to ensure the success of your mentoring program, you must prepare and plan for it carefully. Effective mentoring is more likely to occur when you implement it in a structured manner. Set out expectations and a timeline for your program. The program should also include the necessary resources and guidance to allow your mentees to acquire skills successfully. And it must foster a mutually beneficial mentoring relationship for participants.

You can take a number of steps to ensure that your mentoring program will be successful. For example, you need to ensure your mentoring goals are aligned with the personal goals of the participants. You should carefully select and match participants for the program. And incorporate personal development programs into the mentoring process.

This course covers the steps needed to initiate a mentoring program in your organization. It begins by detailing the elements of a successful mentoring program. It then explains how you can plan the mentoring program. And it concludes by explaining how to establish the mentoring process, including the creation of personal development plans.

SUCCESSFUL MENTORING PROGRAMS

Preparing for a mentoring program

Mentoring is a process that ensures that crucial expertise and knowledge aren't lost with turnover of staff. It entails a professional relationship, usually between two individuals – the mentor and the mentee. Mentors are more experienced individuals who transfer wisdom and expertise to less experienced colleagues, or mentees.

Mentoring has many benefits for organizations. By matching experienced personnel with newer recruits, individual performance can be improved. Mentoring can also strengthen organizational ties and ensure greater continuity of expertise over time.

Reflect

What kinds of preparations do you think you need to make for a mentoring program?

You may have said that your organization's needs should be assessed with a needs analysis. Initially you should determine where the need for mentoring is greatest. A needs analysis can also help you assess what support is available from managers for such a program.

You can carry out your needs analysis by conducting online surveys, focus groups, and individual staff member interviews. Employees can highlight where mentoring is lacking and where they would find it most useful. You could also use data from secondary resources, such as existing productivity assessments.

Those managing mentoring programs should create a task force of between six and eight people who will help set the objectives of the mentoring program.

This task force should be made up of a cross section of staff members from every level of your organization, and should include potential mentors and mentees.

For example, management at an advertising firm has started planning their mentoring program by implementing a needs analysis.

A team conducts interviews with staff members from across the firm's departments. The consensus is that the Sales Department could benefit most from mentoring, as staff members are relatively inexperienced.

Management selects eight employees from across the firm for the mentoring task force, which scrutinizes the needs analysis and decides on the program's mentoring objectives.

Question

What preparations should be made before a mentoring program is created?

Options:

1. A needs analysis should be conducted
2. A mentoring task force should be selected
3. A mentoring budget should be finalized
4. The mentoring participants should be selected

Answer

Option 1: This is a correct option. Conducting a needs analysis is the first thing an organization should do when preparing a mentoring program.

Option 2: This is a correct option. The task force should include between six and eight individuals from across the company who help select mentoring objectives.

Option 3: This is an incorrect option. Although it may be necessary to create a mentoring budget, it usually isn't done at this stage.

Option 4: This is an incorrect option. Participant selection is done during the implementation of the program.

Attracting participants

You've assessed your needs, but how can you guarantee success? There are nine elements that should be planned when creating a successful mentoring program. The first three attract participants. These are a statement of purpose, a recruitment strategy, and an orientation program. The next three organize participants with an eligibility screening program, a curriculum, and a matching strategy. And finally, to deliver results there is a support structure and recognition program, a graduation and closure plan, and an assessment system.

The primary function of the first three elements is attracting participants. You start by writing a statement of purpose to drive the program. You then formulate a recruitment strategy and design an orientation program.

See each element to find out more information.

Statement of purpose

Your statement of purpose sets out where mentoring is needed and establishes the goals of the program from the outset.

For example, a mobile communications firm's mentoring statement of purpose is "This program will give mentees a foundation in the firm's leading-edge research."

Recruitment strategy

Your recruitment strategy should include printed promotional material, e-mails, and informal communications sessions to inform and entice potential participants.

A mobile communications firm's potential participants are all sent a link to an online brochure that shows how they can benefit from the program. To further entice employees, recruitment posters are placed in prominent areas of the employee break room.

Orientation

An orientation program should be created and presented once

mentoring begins. It serves the purpose of clarifying roles, responsibilities, and expectations for mentors and mentees.

A mobile communications firm develops an orientation program that comprises a day of seminars for participants. These seminars introduce both mentors and mentees to the firm's mentoring program and explains how they'll be expected to perform.

Remember the advertising firm? Its mentoring program statement of purpose targets sales personnel, linking experienced sales team members with new recruits, with the goal of orientation and skill enhancement.

To recruit participants, a web site explaining the mentoring program is created and the relevant employees are notified about it by e-mail.

Once both mentors and mentees are recruited, the firm arranges a half-day orientation in which the roles of participants and expected outcomes are explained and participants become better acquainted.

Question

Which examples illustrate actions taken to attract participants that make mentoring more likely to be successful?

Options:

1. An aviation firm's mentoring manager creates a statement of purpose that says "Seeking to retain the knowledge base of near-retirees"
2. A catering firm implements an e-mail campaign aimed at informing employees of the new mentoring program
3. An IT consultancy commissions a cost-benefit analysis to assess whether a mentoring program represents a good use of company resources
4. An afternoon is set aside for a seminar that introduces participants to a retailer's mentoring program
5. A ceramics manufacturer employs a mentoring expert from a sister company to temporarily helm the new

mentoring program

Answer

Option 1: *This is a correct option. Successful mentoring programs are initiated by a statement of purpose that gives the program direction by stating mentoring goals.*

Option 2: *This is a correct option. Mentoring programs that succeed implement a recruitment strategy to attract employees.*

Option 3: *This is an incorrect option. Cost-benefit analyses are not required in a mentoring program and aren't useful for attracting participants.*

Option 4: *This is a correct option. Successful mentoring programs include an orientation program for potential participants.*

Option 5: *This is an incorrect option. Although hiring an outside expert might be useful at the commencement of a mentoring program, it's not required for attracting participants.*

Organizing participants

The next three of the nine elements for planning a successful mentoring program relate to organizing the participants. Not everyone is suited to mentoring, so you need to create an eligibility screening program. A curriculum detailing what the mentoring program will entail is also essential for effective mentoring. However, the foundation of good mentoring is an effective matching strategy.

See each element to find out more information.

Eligibility screening program

An eligibility screening program sets out for mentors and mentees who is eligible for the mentoring program. Eligibility should be tied to the statement of purpose.

For example, a software company precludes senior engineers from being mentees, as they're considered to have the optimum level of expertise.

Curriculum

A training curriculum should be developed for mentors and mentees. This allows them to learn the requirements, goals, policies, and procedures of the mentoring program.

A software company's mentoring manager creates a curriculum for the mentoring program that explains how participants benefit from the mentoring program and how to conduct sessions.

Matching strategy

A matching strategy should be formulated that considers compatibility, interests, and other elements that might impact the mentor's relationship with a potential mentee.

A software company's mentoring manager selects a number of criteria, including technical expertise, current position, and personality to help with matching mentors to mentees.

Consider again the example of the advertising firm. Since the sales team is the target of mentoring, only those who work on the team or who are likely to be placed on it in the future are eligible mentees. Prospective mentors are limited to those with a solid track record in sales.

A document is created that sets out what is expected of each participant over the lifetime of the program. It also details policies and procedures. It explains that mentees' sales figures will be compared from month to month in group meetings. This is to give mentors added impetus to help their mentees.

Next, the mentoring manager sets up a matching strategy. This includes criteria like interests, previous experience, and specific skill sets. These are used for matching each mentor with the most suitable mentee.

Question

Which examples illustrate steps taken to organize participants for successful mentoring?

Options:

1. The mentoring manager at a sports equipment company checks if volunteers are eligible for the company's mentoring program
2. Management at a periodicals publisher creates docu-

ments detailing all the information mentors and mentees might need
3. The mentoring manager at an electricity company
creates a spreadsheet that contains criteria for matching mentors to mentees
4. Management at a produce distributor creates a confidential support system for mentoring participants
5. The mentoring manager at a book publishing firm
picks a task force to help identify mentoring needs in
the firm

Answer

Option 1: This is a correct option. An eligibility screening program is necessary for successfully organizing potential participants in a firm's mentoring program.

Option 2: This is a correct option. Creating a mentoring curriculum helps participants know exactly what's expected of them going forward.

Option 3: This is a correct option. A firm's matching strategy organizes mentors into partnerships with their most suitable mentees.

Option 4: This is an incorrect option. Creating a support system is an action taken when ensuring results will be delivered.

Option 5: This is an incorrect option. Mentoring task forces are selected at the beginning stages of the mentoring program's creation.

Delivering results

It's important to remember mentoring programs are never a short-term set up. They usually last months, sometimes years. The final three of the nine elements for planning a successful mentoring program are about delivering results. Include a support structure and recognition as part of your program. You should also create a graduation and closure plan. And finally, you should establish an assessment system to evaluate the mentoring program.

See each element to find out more information.

Support structure and recognition

Ongoing support for mentors and mentees is important because the process and relationship evolve over time. You may have to help resolve interpersonal difficulties or provide support if mentees' requirements change. You should also establish a recognition and reward plan for mentors and mentees.

For example, a restaurant chain that has a mentoring program forms a dispute resolution committee to solve interpersonal problems among participants.

Graduation and closure plan

To mark the conclusion of your mentoring program, you might decide to organize a graduation ceremony where awards are given to mentors and mentees. Such a ceremony recognizes participants' achievements but also clearly marks the end of the mentoring program.

The restaurant chain sets aside an afternoon for an informal graduation ceremony for mentees.

Assessment system

You need to assess the success of your program. Include a monitoring process that makes sure the matching is effective. Assessments can be made through the use of surveys, questionnaires, and one-on-one interviews with participants.

An assessing committee is created by the restaurant chain. This group meets every quarter to assess the progress of mentors and mentees.

The mentoring manager at the advertising firm knows that both mentors and mentees in the program will face difficulties. The manager creates a support structure, allowing mentors and mentees to voice problems, and providing ground rules for dealing with them. The manager also sets out milestones where the mentors' and mentees' achievements are recognized.

At the end of the program, the mentoring manager organizes an informal graduation ceremony. Speeches are made, lauding the progress of participants from the sales team, and certificates are issued. This helps bring closure for those involved.

Throughout the mentoring program, the manager undertakes

an ongoing assessment. At regular intervals he talks to mentors and mentees about their progress, and about the goals of the program. The manager also makes a final overall evaluation of the program.

Question

Which examples illustrate steps taken to deliver results in a successful mentoring program?

Options:

1. The mentoring manager at a software company selects a support officer who will help mentors and mentees with any issues they may have
2. To mark the conclusion of its mentoring program, an environmental consultancy has a graduation ceremony for participants
3. Managers at a sports academy contact all employees to inform them of the mentoring program being implemented
4. Participants in a financial firm's mentoring program answer regular online questionnaires assessing their progress
5. The mentoring manager at a pharmaceutical company matches potential mentors with their most suitable mentees

Answer

Option 1: *This is a correct option. Implementing a support structure and recognition are ways of ensuring a mentoring program delivers results.*

Option 2: *This is a correct option. A graduation and closure plan rewards participants but also clearly marks the conclusion of the mentoring program.*

Option 3: *This is an incorrect option. A recruitment strategy isn't used when making sure a program delivers results.*

Option 4: *This is a correct option. An assessment program is essential to making sure a mentoring program delivers results.*

Option 5: *This is an incorrect option. A matching strategy is an elem-*

ent of successful mentoring programs but not when assuring delivery of results.

Successful mentoring programs incorporate each of the nine elements. These elements ensure that the mentoring program is well structured from the outset. They also ensure that long-term support and monitoring are provided for the mentoring program. This is for the benefit of mentors, mentees, and, ultimately, the organization.

Question
An insurance firm sets up a mentoring program. It decides where mentoring is needed, and then goals are set out for the program. Staff members are contacted and asked to participate, and soon a seminar is arranged explaining mentoring for participants. Manuals are created with the program's details. Jane, the mentoring manager, encourages mentors and mentees to contact her if they need help. She informs participants of milestones they've achieved. She also monitors the progress of all mentees, organizing regular chats with them. Finally, Jane arranges awards for participants who have successfully completed the program.
Which statement is true of this mentoring program?
Options:
1. The firm has neglected to include an eligibility screening program or matching strategy
2. The firm has included all the elements needed to make this a successful mentoring program
3. The firm has neglected to include orientation or a graduation and closure plan
4. The firm has neglected to include a recruitment strategy and a statement of purpose

Answer
Option 1: *This is the correct option. The program detailed doesn't include a means to identify the eligibility of potential participants. It also doesn't detail how mentors will be matched to mentees.*

Option 2: *This is an incorrect option. An eligibility screening program and matching strategy are missing elements from this scenario.*

Option 3: *This is an incorrect option. The seminar in the scenario is for orientation and the awards mark the graduation and closure plan.*

Option 4: *This is an incorrect option. The recruitment strategy entails contacting staff about participation. The statement of purpose includes where mentoring is needed and the goals of the program.*

Summary

When creating a mentoring program, a needs analysis should be undertaken to identify where mentoring will most benefit the company. This can be done through surveys, focus groups, and interviews with staff members. A task force should also be set up to help establish the parameters of the mentoring program. This should include personnel from across the company, including potential mentors and mentees.

There are nine elements that should be included in a successful mentoring program. The first three of these relate to participant attraction. They are a statement of purpose, a recruitment strategy, and orientation.

The next three elements help ensure successful participation. They are an eligibility screening program, curriculum, and matching strategy.

Finally, in order to deliver results, the last three elements must be included in a mentoring program. These are a support structure and recognition, a graduation and closure plan, and an assessment program.

DESIGNING YOUR MENTORING PROGRAM

Mentoring planning and goals

An effective mentoring program requires planning. Be clear from the outset about what your program's goals are and who will be involved, and design your program with these goals in mind.

There are five steps in designing a mentoring program. To begin, assess the organizational goals you're trying to meet. Once you have that focus, decide how to conduct the mentoring. Next, prepare a curriculum that outlines the program and its procedures. After you've established the curriculum, create an orientation program and then define recruitment and matching criteria.

The first step in designing the program is to define its purpose by assessing organizational goals. Your organization's mentoring goals should be aligned to overall organizational goals, so you must carefully assess the aims of your mentoring program.

This helps ensure that more personnel will buy into the program by making the program more relevant to their organizational needs.

From this assessment, you create a statement of purpose, which clearly explains the program's goals and can be referred to later if uncertainty arises.

An organization may identify a number of mentoring goals.

These could include spreading out expertise, developing job-specific skills, improving staff retention, improving inter-departmental communication, reducing staff isolation, or integrating new recruits.

Take, for example, an insurance firm. Its managers assess the organization's mentoring goals and identify integrating new recruits as the primary goal. A statement of purpose is created that says "New hire mentoring will be used to help new staff members integrate and succeed in the firm." Veteran salespeople mentor new recruits, helping them solve the work issues that all newcomers face.

Question
Why should you assess organizational goals when planning a mentoring program?

Options:

1. It ensures more employees will buy into the mentoring program 2. It contributes toward creating an effective statement of purpose 3. It means that creating a curriculum won't be necessary

4. It ensures that your orientation program will achieve its aims

Answer

Option 1: *This is a correct option. By aligning mentoring with needs, assessing organizational goals makes the mentoring more relevant to employees.*

Option 2: *This is a correct option. Mentoring goals as identified in the assessment are used to create the statement of purpose.*

Option 3: *This is an incorrect option. A curriculum is always needed in a successful mentoring program.*

Option 4: *This is an incorrect option. Although organizational goals are considered when creating an orientation program, the assessment itself has no impact on the efficacy of the program.*

Mentoring types

After setting your mentoring goals, the second step is to decide how mentoring will be conducted. There are four basic types of mentoring: one-on-one mentoring, team mentoring, e-mentoring, and executive mentoring.

See each type of mentoring to find out more information.

One-on-one mentoring

One-on-one mentoring is a relationship between a single mentor and a single mentee. It enables participants to develop a personal relationship, and the mentor can provide individual support to the mentee.

However, one-on-one mentoring is limited by the number of mentors available for a program.

Team mentoring

Team mentoring has a single mentor working with up to six mentees. The team meets regularly to discuss issues, and mentees can also learn from their co-mentees.

One of the limitations of team mentoring is the scheduling problems that can arise when dealing with a large team. It's also less personal than one-on-one mentoring.

E-mentoring

E-mentoring uses online communication as the primary means of interaction, usually supplemented with some real-world meetings. E-mentoring can be useful where there's a significant distance between participants.

While some consider e-mentoring too impersonal, technologies such as instant messaging and social media can allow mentors and mentees to develop rapport.

Executive mentoring

Executive mentoring occurs when the mentor and mentee are both executives in an organization. It's an effective way to prepare up-and-coming executives for the departure of senior colleagues. Executive mentors help their mentees achieve their own insights and self- awareness.

Executive mentoring is limited by the number of executives available to mentor and the various constraints on their time.

Consider a corporate travel agency that implements a mentoring program. It chooses one-on-one mentoring, as its staff members all work in the same offices and individual mentors are available for each mentee. A senior sales team leader, Mary, is selected to mentor a junior sales executive, Scott.

Mary and Scott meet up every second Friday. Mary shows Scott how to build rapport with long-term customers, and how to best satisfy their travel needs.

Mary and Scott form a strong working relationship. Mary knows Scott well enough to be able to vouch for him. Similarly, Scott knows he can rely on Mary to guide him through challenges.

Now consider an example of team mentoring. Travis, a senior account manager, is a mentor at an insurance firm. Heather and Geoff are his mentees. They've recently started on the program, and this is their third meeting. Follow along as they discuss an issue.

Travis: Good to see you guys! How are things going? *Travis is enthusiastic.*

Heather: Pretty well...I guess.

Geoff: Not so good for me. Something's been bothering me. *Geoff is a bit dejected.*

Travis: Well, that's what I'm here for! Lay it on me.

Geoff: There's this client, Phlogistix. I've been assessing their insurance needs. But whenever I call the manager, Nancy, over there, she always wants to talk to someone more senior than me.

Travis: Ah, yes. I had similar problems when I started out. Trust me...if you stay on top of things and show your competence, you'll gain her trust. Eventually, it won't be a problem anymore. *Travis is thoughtful.*

Geoff: Yeah...eventually. But in the meantime, my manager is going to think I can't handle clients as big as Phlogistix if Nancy's constantly contacting him. *Geoff is dejected again.*

Heather: You know what I do when that happens to me? I just tell clients my manager is unavailable, but I can take care of them immediately. Then I say if they still aren't satisfied after talking to me, I'll have my manager call them back. They're usually fine with that and they rarely ask to talk to my manager afterwards. I know it's a little white lie, but my manager is pretty busy most of the time.

Heather is enthusiastic.

Travis: That's not a bad approach – it's a good way to establish your own credibility. And I think we can forgive the little white lie. Good problem solving, Heather!

Travis has a good relationship with his mentees. And Heather offers useful advice. Team mentoring means mentees can rely not just on their mentor, but also on their co-mentees for advice.

Question

What are the advantages of team mentoring?

Options:

1. It allows wider inclusion of mentees when there are relatively few mentors available
2. Mentees can benefit from the guidance of their co-mentees
3. Mentees get more focused attention from mentors
4. Meetings are easier to schedule

Answer

Option 1: This is a correct option. Team mentoring links a single mentor to several mentees, which is useful when potential mentees outnumber mentors.

Option 2: This is a correct option. Mentees will often offer solutions to their co-mentees in team mentoring meetings.

Option 3: This is an incorrect option. Mentors have to necessarily focus less attention on each mentee in team mentoring than in one-on-one mentoring.

Option 4: This is an incorrect option. With the bigger number of participants in team mentoring, it's more likely that schedule problems will occur.

Organizations often choose e-mentoring when they have employees based in different locations. Say, for example, an electronics firm has a mentoring goal of transferring core competencies from its research hub in North America to its manufacturing base in Europe.

Brad, a researcher in North America, is tasked with mentoring Katerina, an engineer at one of the firm's plants. Brad and Katerina regularly exchange e-mails and use instant messaging, and occasionally teleconference.

The e-mentoring is complemented with meetings whenever Brad visits the firm's European plants. These real-world meetings help solidify Brad's e-mentoring.

Consider this example of executive mentoring. Bernard is a partner at a venture capital firm. Kyra is a talented senior executive. Bernard will be retiring next year and is mentoring Kyra, who has been identified as having the potential to fill a key leadership position. Bernard uses their monthly meetings to inform Kyra how he sources investment opportunities. Kyra enjoys hearing his stories and feels she's learning a lot from Bernard's advice and encouragement.

Bernard knows that when he retires, the company will still benefit from his experience through Kyra's mentoring. Kyra in turn knows she'll be able to make informed executive decisions when Bernard is no longer there to advise her.

Question

A biotechnology company's CEO appoints a mentoring manager to implement a mentoring program for junior scientists at the company's European research center. The manager finds there are twice as many applicants for mentee positions than for mentors. The manager would prefer that the program encompass as many participants as feasible.

What is the most suitable mentoring type for this company?

Options:

1. One-on-one mentoring 2. Team mentoring
3. Executive mentoring 4. E-mentoring

Answer

bar

b

Option 1: This option is incorrect. If the mentoring manager implemented one-on-one mentoring, many of the applicants for mentee positions would be excluded.

Option 2: This is the correct option. By creating teams where there are two mentees per mentor, the mentoring manager can include all volunteers in the program.

Option 3: This option is incorrect. Executive mentoring is typically one-on-one and, in this scenario, it is junior scientists who are being mentored, not executives.

Option 4: This option is incorrect. E-mentoring isn't required, as all mentors and mentees will be in the same location.

Curriculum, orientation, and matching

The third step in designing a mentoring program is to prepare a curriculum that explains how mentors build positive relations with mentees. It should also show mentees how they can get the most out of the program. And it should detail policies and procedures pertaining to the program for all participants.

Consider this example. A private academic institution that caters primarily to gifted students implements a mentoring program for its teaching staff. New teachers will be mentored by more senior staff members.

The mentoring program manager compiles a curriculum – a document that includes chapters specifically for mentors, such as "The right mentoring attitude," and "Communication skills for mentors."

It also includes the mentoring program's procedures for both mentors and mentees. So if mentees find they have a problem during the process, they can consult the curriculum to find the correct course of action to address the issue.

Having established a curriculum, the fourth step is to create an orientation program. This enables participants to discuss the goals of the program, and should help answer any questions they have. An orientation program might consist of a meeting, a series of meetings, or even a work retreat. It could include presentations about successful mentoring projects in other departments or firms, or it might simply entail introducing participants to one another.

Consider the private academic institution. Its orientation program comprises an afternoon meeting, which all mentors and mentees attend, when classes have concluded for the week.

The mentoring program manager and another speaker, a teacher who has been involved in mentoring before, give presentations explaining the program overview, the benefits participants may derive from the project, and the expected level of commitment.

The program manager concludes with a short presentation on the mentoring program policies, including expected deliverables, mediation policy, withdrawal policy, and other details relevant to the mentoring program.

Question

Match the examples to the corresponding steps in the mentoring process. Each step may have more than one match.

Options:

1. Mike, the mentoring program manager at a retail firm, organizes events to introduce the program to participants
2. The mentoring manager at a logistics firm, Joan, convenes a meeting where participants are told about the program
3. An appliance retailer's mentoring managers create a booklet that gives participants the information they need to proceed
4. Ayana, the mentoring program manager at a clothing firm, creates a document that mentors and mentees can use to guide them

Targets:

1. Create an orientation program
2. Prepare a curriculum

Answer

Orientation can take the form of a series of events or a single meeting

that lets participants get acquainted with the process.
A mentoring program's curriculum is a document or booklet pro-
vided to participants with relevant information on the program.

Your final step in developing the mentoring program is to
define recruitment and matching criteria. You need to recruit
the most suitable candidates for your mentoring program. You
then have to match up mentors and mentees in the most effective way. Gather information up front about participants by implementing an eligibility screening program. Then you need to
design a matching system that matches mentees to mentors by
personality, interests, and other elements.

An organization's eligibility screening program helps identify
those most suited to mentoring and those who would benefit
most. You should ask potential mentors about their skills, level
of education, occupation, and professional experience.

Someone outside the group of potential mentors and mentees,
such as the program manager, determines the suitable matches,
based upon the matching criteria.

Matching criteria, such as the participants' skill sets, interests,
previous work experience, and levels of education, are used to
pair mentors and mentees.

The private academic institute decides to implement an eligibility screening program for participants in the mentoring program.

Those without extensive teaching experience are automatic-
ally discounted from being mentors. Similarly, a number of potential mentees are disqualified, as they're deemed to already
have sufficient experience.

Once the screening process ends, the mentoring manager starts
selecting potential matches for the program. Where possible,
the manager gives each mentee two or more suitable mentors to
choose from.

Reflect
Now that you've learned the steps to developing a mentoring

program, why do you think preparing and planning for mentoring in your organization is important?

The importance of preparing and planning for mentoring

As you may have noted, by preparing and planning for mentoring, your program is more likely to align with organizational goals for mentoring.

Also, the mentoring relationship has a better chance of being successful if the correct preparations are made, making sure the matching criteria and procedure are adhered to.

Question

Gail, a senior manager, has been tasked with designing a mentoring program for her IT firm, which operates from multiple locations.

Match each step in designing the mentoring program to its example.

Options:

A. Decide how to conduct the mentoring

B. Prepare a curriculum

C. Create an orientation program

D. Define recruitment and matching criteria for mentors and mentees

Targets:

1. Gail decides that one-on-one mentoring will be used primarily, supplemented by e-mentoring
2. Gail compiles a document that defines how succession mentoring will be achieved and the guidelines for conducting mentoring
3. Gail organizes a seminar that outlines the goals of succession mentoring and provides an open forum for discussion of the program
4. Gail interviews prospective participants to determine whether they're suitable, then uses data from the interviews to match mentors to mentees

Answer

There are many ways to conduct mentoring, but here one-on-one mentoring and e-mentoring are complementary choices.

Preparing a curriculum informs mentees on how they can get the most out of a program and details policies and procedures.

Orientation programs enable participants to discuss the goals of the program and get their queries answered.

Defining recruitment and matching criteria helps you find the most suitable candidates for your mentoring program.

Mentoring matches

How well mentors and mentees are matched is the ultimate consideration when designing your mentoring program. A mentoring relationship usually lasts months, sometimes even years, so compatibility is important. When a mentor and mentee are well matched, it's to their mutual satisfaction, and the mentor is likely to impart guidance that will be of more help to the mentee. And the mentee should be comfortable asking the mentor any questions that arise during the process.

Mentoring matches usually work best when the participants are allowed to choose each other. In contrast, when participants feel coerced into a relationship, the matches are often unsuccessful.

However, mentees shouldn't be given an unguided choice of mentor. They're likely to pick a mentor they already know and get along well with, or a high performer within the organization. The scope for learning experiences may be narrowed between friends, and selecting a high performer might give the mentee unrealistic expectations for the mentoring experience. Giving the mentee a narrow choice of suitable mentors is probably the best way of facilitating effective matching.

An effective matching strategy contains four elements. Include an explicit link to the program's statement of purpose. You should also include commitment on the part of the mentor and the mentee. Next, include appropriate criteria for the matches. And finally, include a contract signed by both parties that states they agree to the conditions of the match and the relationship. Criteria for matches include participants' skills, career interests, levels of education, motivations for volunteering, and temperaments.

This information is acquired from participants via interviews, focus groups, or online and offline forms.

Question
What's the best means by which a mentee should be paired with a mentor?
Options:
1. Mentees should be given a choice between a few suitable mentors 2. Mentees should be assigned a mentor
3. Mentees should be allowed to pick any mentor they want
Answer
Option 1: *This is the correct option. While some choice should exist, mentees should be guided in whom they pick.*
Option 2: *This is an incorrect option. Imposing a mentor on a mentee may result in a negative mentoring experience.*
Option 3: *This is an incorrect option. Mentees may pick someone they know well or an overachiever, either of whom might be unsuitable.*

Mentoring compatibility
The success of a mentoring partnership often hinges on compatibility, which is ensured by matching criteria such as personality, accessibility, rank and position, expertise, work style, and demographics.
See each criterion to learn more about it.

Personality
Some people have an instant personal connection that makes a lasting mentoring bond more likely. In contrast, personality clashes can doom a mentoring relationship. Some people are serious in their conduct, while others enjoy humor. Sociability is another aspect of personality that varies.
For example, at a telesales company, a mentor and mentee get along very well. Both have a similar sense of humor so their mentoring relationship goes well.

Accessibility

To be well matched, mentors and mentees must be accessible to each other. If participants are in the same location, it makes it easier for them to develop a good match. If they're not, they can still develop a good match by making time for each other.

For example, at a financial firm, a potential mentor and mentee pairing had to be canceled. Their schedules were incompatible, so they were unable to meet up regularly.

Rank and position

Within an organization's hierarchy, the mentor shouldn't be in a supervisory position over the mentee. This may lead to conflict. However, there's no reason mentors shouldn't be ranked significantly higher than their mentees within the organization.

At a bank, mentees are deliberately selected from a different department than their mentors, to avoid supervisory conflicts.

Expertise

Matching expertise entails matching up mentees' desired skills and interests with mentors who will be able to provide guidance in those areas.

At an IT firm, for instance, a mentee who's keen on learning about the new servers is paired with the mentor who implemented the server architecture.

Work style

Different people have different work styles. It's important to match up mentors and mentees whose work styles fit together.

Consider a cleaning products manufacturer. Its mentoring manager matches a very hands-on mentor with a similarly styled mentee.

Demographics

Your organization's mentoring program should include a diverse group of people across gender, race, and other demographics, but should also be a fair representation of the staff.

For example, a communications firm's matching strategy deliberately mixes genders and social backgrounds. The mentoring manager feels that this will make for more effective mentoring relationships.

Mentors may need to adapt their work styles to their mentees, so they must decide whether they're willing to do this.

It's also important that both parties are clear about what they expect from the relationship. If either party has unrealistic expectations, it can damage the relationship.

Consider the example of Celeste and Jenna, a mentor and mentee at a logistics company. They're from quite different backgrounds but attended the same university. Celeste admires Jenna's drive, as it reminds her of herself at the same age, and they interact well. They both work at the same office, so they meet regularly. Celeste is quite high up in the company, but she isn't Jenna's boss. The match works very well.

Matching people is crucial to a successful mentoring program. The better matched your participants are, the more likely it is they'll achieve their mentoring goals.

Matching is sometimes implemented using dedicated software that sorts mentors and mentees by the different criteria. This is particularly useful for larger companies dealing with big groups of participants.

Question

A television production company has implemented a mentoring program. Review the mentor
and mentee profiles in the learning aid Mentoring in a Television Production Company .

Match each of the mentees to their most suitable mentor.

Options:

A. Angus B. Valerie C. Bob

Targets:

1. Verne 2. William 3. Mindy

Answer

Verne is best matched to Angus, as their interests match the closest and Verne's expertise would benefit Angus the most.

William is best matched to Valerie, as their personalities suit each

other and William's experience would most benefit Valerie.
Mindy is best matched to Bob, as Mindy's preferred method of mentoring would suit Bob's personality. Her expertise line up well too.

Summary

There are five steps in designing a company's mentoring program. First, assess organizational goals. Second, decide how to conduct the mentoring. Third, prepare a curriculum. Fourth, create an orientation program. And fifth, define recruitment and matching criteria for mentors and mentees.

There are four primary types of mentoring an organization may use: one-on-one mentoring, team mentoring, e-mentoring, and executive mentoring.

The criteria used to ensure compatibility include personality, accessibility, rank and position, expertise, work style, and demographics.

ESTABLISHING THE MENTORING PROCESS

Stages of mentoring

Mentoring relationships can last for months, even years, and go through distinct stages during that time. A long-term commitment from mentors and mentees is needed to maximize the benefits of the mentoring experience.

There are three stages of the mentoring process. Stage one typically lasts up to six months. The middle period, stage two, usually lasts between 6 and 18 months. And stage three, the winding down period, is usually reached after 24 months.

See each stage to find out more information.

Stage 1

Stage one of the mentoring process is primarily about setting the direction of the mentoring and building rapport between participants. Responsibilities are also established.

The mentor and mentee set the direction by agreeing on desired outcomes and how these are to be achieved. This links the objectives of the mentoring process to day-to-day activities. Rapport building ensures a mutual trust and goodwill between the participants.

Stage 2

The core phase of the mentoring process is stage two.

In this stage, the mentor provides support for the mentee by enquiring about, challenging, and analyzing the mentee's actions and opinions. As the stage progresses, the mentee becomes more and more independent from the mentor.

Stage 3

Stage three is where the mentoring process is eventually wrapped up.

By the conclusion of stage three, mentees are confident and able enough to proceed on their own. This stage is crucial, as it prevents an unhealthy dependency forming on the part of the mentee.

This topic focuses on stage one. The mentoring relationship is established during this stage.

Question

What are the key elements of stage one of the mentoring process?

Options:

1. Rapport building between mentors and mentees 2. Direction setting

3. Winding down the relationship

4. Challenging the mentee's opinions

5. Establishing responsibilities Answer

Option 1: This option is correct. For the mentoring relationship to thrive, mentors and mentees need to build rapport in stage one.

Option 2: This option is correct. By setting the direction of the mentoring in stage one, both mentors and mentees know the desired outcomes and how to achieve them in the later stages.

Option 3: This option is incorrect. Winding down the mentoring relationship is a key component of stage three.

Option 4: This option is incorrect. The mentor challenges the mentee's opinions on various issues in stage two, not stage one.

Option 5: This option is correct. Establishing responsibilities is a primary purpose of stage one.

Direction setting

There are several key activities participants undertake when establishing a mentoring relationship. These include setting the direction, building rapport, and establishing responsibilities.

SORIN DUMITRASCU

The first activity involves setting the direction of the mentoring. Mentors and mentees work together to map out the path for the process that will lead to mentees fulfilling their learning goals.

The first mentoring meetings are taken up with several activities. To set the direction for a mentee, you need to plan an outline of expectations, roles, and duties. Then identify learning needs and objectives and ascertain preferred learning styles. You must also plan the details of future meetings and define learning activities for accomplishing goals and objectives. Finally, exchange contact details with your mentee.

See each activity to find out more about it.

Outline expectations, roles, and duties

Mentors and mentees should be clear about what they can expect from the mentoring process. They should be aware of their duties and roles.

For example, a mentor might print up a document with an outline for the mentee to review.

Identify learning needs and objectives

The mentor works with the mentee to establish where learning should occur. They also identify what the mentee seeks to learn during the relationship.

For example, mentees in a firm might want to learn how to engage customers better, or the details of a technical process.

Identify preferred learning styles

Different people learn in different ways. Mentees must make clear to their mentors the learning style they find most effective.

For example, some mentees learn best by trying something, while others learn best by observing the mentor.

Plan future meetings

Participants plan out the content of future meetings and a workable timetable for them. In a busy working environment, set aside time in advance for mentoring meetings.

For example, a mentor might work with a mentee on producing

a timetable of monthly meetings, with a provisional theme for each meeting.

Identify learning activities

Mentors help mentees select various activities that will help them achieve their learning needs and objectives.

Mentors might, for example, set out a program of work tasks that the mentees must complete before their next meeting. These tasks would be tailored to help the mentees reach their learning goals.

Exchange contact details

Mentors and mentees exchange e-mail addresses and phone numbers to allow for ease of contact in the future.

The mentor spends the next few meetings helping the mentee develop information from the direction-setting activities into a personal development plan. This is a document that mentees create, which will contain all relevant information generated during mentoring.

Personal development plans detail mentees' mentoring objectives, and activities through which they'll achieve the desired outcomes. Mentors and managers may contribute to the plan with analysis and suggestions.

Think of the personal development plan as a contract between the mentor and the mentee. It's common for both mentors and mentees to sign the plan. Objectives in the personal development plan should align with the mentee's manager's objectives and wider business objectives.

The personal development plan is crucial to direction setting, as it lays out clearly where the mentoring is taking the mentee and what the mentee's obligations are in relation to the process.

Pam, the head of new business at an aviation firm, is mentoring Enrique, a business analyst. At their first meeting, Pam talks to Enrique about what they both can expect from the relationship. They discuss each other's roles and the duties Enrique is expected to perform in the coming months.

They then discuss Enrique's learning needs. Enrique informs

Pam that he would particularly like to learn how to evaluate alternative business ideas. His goal is to be able to provide management with solid analyses of existing opportunities.

They step through Enrique's learning style. He tells Pam he learns best from observing others work. With this in mind, Pam arranges for Enrique to shadow her while she attends business meetings. He'll take notes on the experience for discussion in their meetings.

Pam and Enrique agree to a schedule of further meetings, to be held on a monthly basis, and exchange contact details.

At their next meeting, Pam and Enrique work on Enrique's personal development plan, which includes the details of their previous activities. It also includes a mentoring agreement, outlining their obligations, which they both sign.

Over the coming months, Enrique will use this personal development plan to help him gauge whether he's fulfilling his obligations and achieving his learning objectives.

Question

What are the steps to set direction for the mentoring process?

Options:

1. Outline expectations, roles, and duties 2. Identify learning needs and objectives 3. Ascertain preferred learning styles
4. Liaise with management
5. Define learning activities 6. Exchange contact details 7. Create a rewards system 8. Plan future meetings

Answer

Option 1: *This option is correct. Mentors and mentees need to be clear about what they can expect from mentoring and what their roles are.*

Option 2: *This option is correct. To set the direction of the mentoring, it's crucial that the mentee's learning needs and ultimate goals are identified early on.*

Option 3: *This option is correct. As there are numerous ways in which mentees may learn, it's important to be clear which styles they feel best suit them.*

Option 4: This option is incorrect. Although there may be reason at some point to communicate with management, it's not a necessary direction-setting step.

Option 5: This option is correct. To get mentees fulfilling their learning needs, selecting learning activities is another crucial direction-setting activity.

Option 6: This option is correct. There are plenty of occasions outside the scheduled meetings where mentors and mentees may need to communicate.

Option 7: This option is incorrect. Instituting a formal system of rewards isn't a typical direction-setting activity, though it may occur in the later stages of mentoring.

Option 8: This option is correct. In a busy working environment it's necessary to set aside time in advance, and also to plan how this time will be spent.

Rapport building

It's essential for mentors and mentees to establish rapport so the mentoring relationship is productive. Rapport building is the second key activity undertaken in stage one of the mentoring process.

But what exactly is rapport? It's an emotional or intellectual connection between two people. With time and effort, it can be built into a trusting, mutually supportive relationship. Although some mentors and mentees enjoy a natural rapport, others have to work at building it.

To build rapport, it's important that mentors and mentees have positive contact from the beginning.

Small talk can be used by participants to put each other at ease. Eventually this small talk can be built upon, to allow for the discussion of more important issues.

Mentors and mentees should seek common ground, such as shared interests, backgrounds, aspirations, and so on. Common ground allows them to communicate more comfortably.

Regular contact is another way the mentor and mentee can build rapport.

They should lay out a schedule for regular, frequent meetings. These could be on a weekly, or perhaps monthly basis.

Question

Mutual confidentiality is another ingredient in rapport building.

How important do you think confidentiality is in a mentoring relationship?

Options:

1. Very important
2. Somewhat important
3. Not important

Answer

Option 1: *You say that confidentiality is very important in a mentoring relationship. Confidentiality assures the mentee opens up to the mentor, which is essential for rapport building.*

Option 2: *You say that confidentiality is somewhat important in a mentoring relationship. You should remember that confidentiality is a significant component of trust, without which the mentoring relationship won't blossom.*

Option 3: *You say that confidentiality is not important. However, most mentoring relationships are built on a connection established through mutual trust. Trust can only exist when confidentiality is assured.*

Remember Pam and Enrique at the aviation firm? They've already met briefly, but now it's time for their initial mentoring meeting. Follow along as Pam works to build rapport with Enrique.

Pam: Good morning Enrique. Good to see you again. *Pam is friendly.*

Enrique: Good morning, um, Pam. Good to see you too. *Enrique is nervous.*

Pam: There's no reason to be nervous. I remember when I was being mentored. It was five years ago, but I was so nervous! Well, don't worry about the mentoring process – it's a breeze. If you've got any questions, don't hesitate to ask. And of course, anything we talk about is in the strictest confidence.

Enrique: Oh, that's good to know. *Enrique is less nervous.*

Pam: So I'm told you worked at our Tokyo location for a while. That must have been pretty exciting.

Enrique: Oh yes it was. Um, I love traveling and exploring different cultures so it was a great opportunity. It's kind of why I got into this business.

Enrique is much less nervous now.

Pam: You and me both! And what is it you'd like to take away from this mentoring experience? Let's have a look at your development plan.

Enrique: Hmm...well, I want to become a top-rate aviation business analyst! But I suppose my main goal is acquiring ways to evaluate new business. I feel it's a weak point in my abilities.

Pam: Being able to assess one's weaknesses is an admirable trait. Anyway, I don't think we'll have any problem getting along. Let's meet up every Friday at 2:00 p.m. over the next couple of months and we can work on you becoming an even better analyst!

By using ample small talk, assuring confidentiality, and showing the common ground between them, Pam has built rapport with Enrique.

She has also asked friendly, easy, open questions that have helped Enrique feel calmer and more communicative. And she has set up a regular contact schedule.

Question
What are some ways of building rapport during mentoring?
Options:
1. Assuring confidentiality
2. Making small talk
3. Making regular contact
4. Identifying learning styles
5. Being flexible
Answer

Option 1: This is a correct option. In order to build rapport, mentees must trust their mentors. Confidentiality is a big part of that trust.

Option 2: This is a correct option. By making small talk, the mentor puts the mentee at ease so they can make a connection.

Option 3: This is a correct option. In order to build up their personal relationship, mentors and

mentees need regular contact.

Option 4: This is an incorrect option. Identifying learning styles is an action related to direction setting, not rapport building.

Option 5: This is an incorrect option. Being flexible is a mentee's responsibility, not a means of building rapport.

Establishing responsibilities

Establishing responsibilities is the third key activity undertaken in stage one of the mentoring process. Mentors and mentees both have several responsibilities when it comes to making the mentoring partnership work. It's important to establish these from the outset.

The mentor has several responsibilities. Mentors should clarify roles for their mentees and provide an informal atmosphere for the mentoring. It's also important to show empathy for the mentee. And last but not least, the mentor must be positive about the mentee's progress.

See each responsibility to find out more information.

Clarify roles

Mentors need to clarify both their roles and those of their mentees. They must make sure that they don't take on other roles in their mentees' lives. A mentor shouldn't be a counselor, a coach, or a confidante.

Consider Pam and Enrique. Pam states clearly that she only has time for mentoring and can't be there to deal with Enrique's day-to-day issues.

Provide an informal atmosphere

For the mentoring relationship to develop, it needs an informal atmosphere. It's the mentor's responsibility to provide this atmosphere by avoiding formalities and being friendly.

Pam makes sure that some of her meetings with Enrique take place in the canteen and other areas with a less formal atmosphere.

Show empathy

Mentees need to know that mentors empathize with them. Mentors should make it clear that they understand what mentees are going through, as they've faced similar challenges themselves.

Pam regularly reminds Enrique that she was originally a business analyst and understands the pressure he's under.

Be positive

When the mentor has a positive attitude and outlook, the mentee's experience is more likely to be similarly positive.

Pam avoids being overly critical of Enrique when he makes mistakes. Instead she concentrates on how Enrique can benefit by learning from his errors.

The mentee also has a number of responsibilities. Mentees must strive to be honest about all relevant information concerning issues to be resolved. They must also clarify their development needs and be flexible.

For example, Enrique realizes that if he's not being honest about his problems, it will be impossible for Pam to help him solve them.

Enrique must also clarify his needs with regard to the mentoring process. Pam isn't a mind reader, so Enrique should be open and clear as to what direction he needs the mentoring to go in.

As the head of new business, Pam has a more hectic schedule than Enrique. Enrique must accept this and be flexible with regard to meeting arrangements.

Case Study: Question 1 of 3

Scenario

For your convenience, the case study is repeated with each question.

An auto superstore has introduced a mentoring program, and

mentors and mentees have been paired up.

Determine if the guidelines for establishing a mentoring relationship have been correctly applied by answering the questions in order.

Question

Due to a certain lack of direction setting, Justin finds he isn't learning as much as he could from the mentoring relationship with Ryan.

How could the direction setting in this scenario be improved?

Options:

1. Ryan could ask Justin what style of learning most suits him 2. They could identify what Justin wants to learn

3. Ryan and Justin could plan future meetings

4. They could select activities for Justin to help him learn

5. Ryan could outline expectations, roles, and duties for Justin

Answer

Option 1: *This option is correct. Ryan neglects to identify Justin's preferred learning style, so his instruction, although well intended, is ineffective for Justin.*

Option 2: *This option is incorrect. In the scenario, Ryan has worked with Justin on identifying his learning needs and objectives.*

Option 3: *This option is incorrect. A timetable of meetings with proposed themes is set out in the scenario.*

Option 4: *This option is correct. To help set direction, Ryan should help Justin identify learning activities he can do.*

Option 5: *This option is incorrect. In the scenario, Ryan has already outlined expectations, roles, and duties to his mentee Justin.*

Case Study: Question 2 of 3

Scenario

For your convenience, the case study is repeated with each question.

An auto superstore has introduced a mentoring program, and mentors and mentees have been paired up.

Determine if the guidelines for establishing a mentoring relationship have been correctly applied by answering the questions in order.

Question

Justin doesn't feel comfortable explaining his problem to Ryan, as they haven't built up much of a rapport.

How could the rapport building in this scenario be improved?

Options:

1. Ryan could engage in more small talk with Justin 2. Their meetings could be conducted more formally 3. They could meet with more frequency

Answer

Option 1: This is the correct option. Ryan comes across to Justin as aloof. Some small talk might bridge the gap between them.

Option 2: This option is incorrect. Ryan is already formal with Justin, and formality tends to limit the extent to which rapport can be built.

Option 3: This option is incorrect. They've set up a timetable of weekly meetings, so they're already in frequent contact.

Case Study: Question 3 of 3

Scenario

For your convenience, the case study is repeated with each question.

An auto superstore has introduced a mentoring program, and mentors and mentees have been paired up.

Determine if the guidelines for establishing a mentoring relationship have been correctly applied by answering the questions in order.

Question

How could Ryan, as a mentor, improve this mentoring relationship?

Options:

1. Ryan could have more empathy
2. Ryan could be more positive
3. Ryan could provide a more relaxed atmosphere for the mentoring 4. Ryan could clarify their roles

Answer

Option 1: This option is incorrect. Ryan states to Justin that he understands the mentee's difficulties, as he was once a mentee himself.

Option 2: *This option is correct. By being negative, he's failing to build the mentoring relationship properly.*

Option 3: *This option is correct. By acting formally, Ryan has potentially undermined his relationship with Justin.*

Option 4: *This option is incorrect. Ryan clarified their roles from the outset in this scenario.*

Summary

There are three stages to the mentoring process. Stage one encompasses the first six months. Stage two typically lasts between 6 and 18 months. Stage three is reached after 24 months usually. Stage one involves setting the direction, building rapport, and establishing responsibilities.

Direction setting entails several activities. In initial meetings, mentors and mentees plan an outline of expectations, roles, and duties. They identify learning needs and objectives and define preferred learning styles. They plan the details of future meetings and identify learning activities for accomplishing goals and objectives. And they exchange contact details. This information is included in the mentee's personal development plan.

Rapport building entails participants finding a connection with each other and building upon this to create a trusting, lasting relationship. Making small talk and identifying common ground are ways of building rapport. Regular meetings are also important.

Mentoring entails a number of responsibilities on the part of mentors and mentees. Mentors must clarify roles for the mentee, provide an informal atmosphere, and show empathy for the mentee. They must also be positive about the mentee's progress. Mentees should be honest, clarify needs, and be flexible.

ESSENTIAL MENTORING TECHNIQUES: BUILDING AND MAINTAINING MENTORING RELATIONSHIPS

Just like any other relationship, mentoring relationships have their share of problems and challenges. It's important to continually monitor the effectiveness of a mentoring relationship to ensure these challenges are resolved.

Although the mentee drives the growth phase of the mentoring relationship, the mentor maintains the bond by effectively understanding, gauging, probing, and responding to the mentee's issues. This is an essential part of maintaining a solid mentor-mentee bond.

Because of the impact on organizational outcomes, this building and maintaining of mentoring relationships is essential. The success of a mentoring relationship depends on the quality of the partnership and organizational support. A relationship's momentum is sustained through things like giving feedback and dealing with personality issues.

There are some basic guidelines the mentor should follow to ensure effective relationship management – for example, letting the mentee set the agenda. It's possible for program coordinators to avoid program-related problems by carefully matching mentors and mentees, planning the program properly, supporting the participants, and minimizing bureaucracy.

However, effective program and planning design can't ensure that problems won't emerge. Possible problems may include a lack of rapport, unrealistic expectations, a lack of commitment, dependency, and negative reactions from others.

In this course, you'll learn how, as a mentor, to manage a mentoring relationship and respond appropriately to issues that arise. The course will also show you how to give constructive feedback that enables mentees to solve their own problems. It then provides guidelines for program coordinators on how to deal with program issues such as too much formality and too little support. And it explains how to address interpersonal issues in order to sustain a valuable mentoring relationship.

MANAGING THE MENTORING RELATIONSHIP AND GIVING FEEDBACK

Managing relationships

Mentoring relationships are long term and require ongoing effort. Establishing a mentoring relationship is just the beginning. It must then be nurtured and maintained. Otherwise, it won't achieve its goal – to foster competence and independence in the mentee.

Mentoring involves a number of stages. The beginning of a mentoring relationship is stage one, the middle is stage two, and the end is stage three.

See each stage in order to find out more about it.

Stage 1

Stage one is the beginning of the relationship. Typically lasting for up to six months, it's primarily about building rapport and setting direction.

Stage 2

Stage two is the middle phase of the relationship. Beginning after 6 months at the latest, it generally lasts for between 6 and 18 months.

The mentor isn't actively involved in the mentee's tasks, but acts as a sounding board during this stage. The mentor inquires, challenges, and analyzes.

Stage 3

Stage three represents the gradual winding down of the relationship. It starts after around 24 months, and lasts for around 6 months.

At the end of this stage, the mentee is independent and self-reliant.

In this course, you'll learn about stage two, when the relationship is nurtured and maintained. This is essential to creating a supportive learning environment – an important part of effective mentoring. Nurturing and maintaining a mentoring relationship entails respect, trust, and open communication.

There must be respect in a mentoring relationship. This ensures effective engagement and mutual understanding.

Trust is another crucial quality for the relationship. Trust must be built over time – and continuously. To build trust, be open, genuine, truthful, and consistent. Trust also depends on both the mentor and the mentee respecting the confidentiality of anything discussed during sessions.

Open communication is the best way to avoid conflict and misunderstandings. Conflict arises more often from misunderstandings or differences in style than from disagreements, which is why communication is important.

The mentor must effectively manage the relationship, and both mentor and mentee must work together to maintain it to their mutual benefit. Effective management involves letting the mentee drive the relationship, ensuring program awareness, helping the mentee build a network, and keeping records.

See each guideline to find out more about it.

Letting mentee drive the relationship

A mentoring relationship should revolve around the mentee's requirements, so it's important to let the mentee drive the relationship. The mentor should listen, encourage, and be positive, but shouldn't dictate what the mentee does.

Driving the relationship means the mentee defines the agenda, and – guided by the mentor – decides the issues to be addressed within the relationship. Instead of being directly involved in the mentee's projects, the mentor's role is as a sounding board – giving opinions and feedback.

Ensuring program awareness

The mentor needs to ensure program awareness among other employees, including the mentee's direct colleagues. This means ensuring everyone understands the program's purpose.

If the purpose of the relationship isn't commonly known, the mentee's colleagues may engage in gossip and speculation, which could fuel resentment or jealousy.

Helping mentee build network

The mentor should help the mentee build a network of contacts. With the mentor's help, the mentee can develop a useful network that could otherwise take years to build.

Mentors can draw on their own network of contacts to aid the mentoring process in situations where the mentor doesn't have the specific skills or experience needed.

Keeping records

Keeping records of mentoring sessions is an important part of effective management of the relationship.

After a mentoring session, the mentor should note the main issues and actions dealt with during that session. It's also a good idea to maintain a record of agreed agendas for later review. The mentor might also note any issues that haven't been addressed, but might be appropriate for future discussion.

Penny, a senior partner at an accounting firm, is an expert in regulatory compliance. For the past six months, she's been mentoring Edward, an associate at the firm, who's doing work in this area for clients. Consider how Penny manages the mentoring relationship.

Because Edward's already reasonably competent in compliance, Penny avoids being too instructive. Instead she lets Edward determine the agenda during sessions. She's also careful not to stifle Edward's development, so she gives guidance and advice when asked, but allows him to make his own judgments. Because it's unusual for an employee to have such access to a senior partner, Penny lets others know about the purpose of the relationship. She doesn't want others to feel Edward is being treated favorably.

During industry events they attend, Penny introduces Edward to her contacts, encouraging him to develop relationships with these people and develop a network of contacts. Finally, Penny keeps detailed accounts of their sessions. She notes the issues discussed, and any proposed solutions. She'll review these records with Edward toward the end of the relationship.

Penny's management of the relationship is effective. In allowing him to determine the agenda, she's letting Edward drive the relationship. By being transparent, she's ensuring program awareness. She's also helping Edward build a network by introducing him to her contacts. Finally, she's keeping records.

Question

Peter, a marketing graduate, has been working in a junior marketing role for a hospitality company for a year. Although he lacks experience, the firm's executives think he would make an excellent regional marketing manager. As part of the process to groom him for this position, Gwen, a senior marketing executive in the company, has been acting as his mentor for about six months. Gwen's assisting Peter with the design of a marketing plan for one of the company's subsidiaries.

What would constitute effective management by Gwen?

Options:

1. Gwen tells Peter to conduct a target market demographic analysis for the subsidiary, and gives detailed instructions on how to do it

2. To avoid causing jealously among other graduate employees, Gwen instructs Peter to keep their relationship confidential

3. As Gwen isn't familiar with the market that Peter's

compiling the plan for, she introduces him to Roy, who's very experienced with this market
4. After each mentoring session with Peter, Gwen makes notes on the issues discussed

Answer

Option 1: *This option is incorrect. Gwen should let Peter drive the relationship as much as possible, rather than dictating what he does.*

Option 2: *This option is incorrect. Gwen should ensure there's program awareness among other employees so that others don't get the wrong idea about the relationship.*

Option 3: *This option is correct. By introducing Peter to a contact who can help him, Gwen's effectively managing the relationship.*

Option 4: *This option is correct. Keeping records of mentoring sessions, as Gwen's doing, is an important part of effective management of the mentoring relationship.*

Giving feedback

It's important to maintain momentum in a mentoring relationship. This can be achieved using meaningful feedback. When given and received correctly, feedback can strengthen the mentoring relationship. Mentees should be instructed to make regular and specific requests for feedback and avoid being defensive. See each mentee guideline to find out more about it.

Make regular and specific requests

Mentees need to be encouraged to regularly ask for detailed feedback. A request for feedback must be specific, clear, and descriptive, ensuring the mentor fully understands what's wanted.

For example, the mentee might ask the mentor for feedback on the approach taken in a specific assignment, and ask for views on alternative approaches.

Avoid being defensive

Although it's normal to react strongly to feedback, it must be made clear to mentees that they should avoid being defensive or responding with denial or resistance. Feedback should instead be seen as an opportunity to integrate new learning.

For instance, if a mentee receives constructive criticism, the mentee should take time to reflect on this, instead of taking it personally or as an attack.

Question

What do you think would be appropriate comments from a mentee when looking for and reacting to feedback?

Options:

1. "In terms of the approach I took to this problem, could you tell me where I did well and where I could have done better?"
2. "It seems from your feedback that you haven't really grasped what my project's all about. You're commenting on something you don't understand."
3. "It's really great to be able to get feedback from someone with so much experience. I'd love to hear some now. Do you have any feedback to give me?"
4. "To be honest, I'm a little disheartened, but I know that if I take your remarks on board, they'll help me improve."

Answer

Option 1: This option is correct. This is an example of asking for feedback, which is good practice for mentees.

Option 2: This option is incorrect. Mentees should avoid responding defensively. Feedback should be taken as an opportunity to integrate new learning.

Option 3: This option is incorrect. Requests for feedback should be specific, giving the mentor full understanding. This request is vague and unclear.

Option 4: This option is correct. Although it's natural to find critical feedback disheartening, it's important not to react defensively but to view it as an opportunity to improve.

Mentors can use several guidelines when giving feedback. Mentors should follow the mentee's agenda, give practical feedback, check for understanding, and make a connection between progress and the bigger picture.

See each guideline to find out more about it.

Follow mentee's agenda

It's important that a mentor follows the mentee's agenda when giving feedback, making it directly relevant and applicable to the mentee's interests and concerns.

The mentor shouldn't attempt to divert the issue, and needs to ensure that the mentee retains ownership of the issue throughout.

Give practical feedback

A mentor should give practical feedback or feedback that can be acted on. Abstract or theoretical feedback has limited value.

It's sometimes a good idea for the mentor to draw on personal experiences that give things another perspective. This mentor could say something like, "I had the same problem once. What I did was..."

Check for understanding

When giving feedback, a mentor should check for understanding of what's being said.

This requires the mentor to actively listen to what the mentee's saying and ask questions to clarify, confirm, and ensure understanding.

Make a connection

When providing feedback, a mentor should always make connections between the progress being made and the ultimate learning objective, between the mentoring journey and the company's business objectives, or between receiving feedback and achieving goals.

This means helping the mentee see feedback as progress toward the ultimate goal – not as an interruption or deviation from the journey.

Remember Penny and Edward at the accounting firm? Edward has recently compiled an internal report outlining basic guidelines on regulatory compliance. He did this in response to a request from Frank, his direct manager. Before releasing the document, which will be distributed to all employees, he asks Penny for feedback.

Follow along as Penny responds to Edward's request for feedback.

Edward: I'm wondering about the guidelines I put together. What do you think? Have I hit the mark?

Edward is enthusiastic.

Penny: Well, I'm not so sure. You know the saying..."a little knowledge is a dangerous thing." You know what I mean?

Penny is cryptic.

Edward: Well, no, I'm not sure I do. *Edward is confused.*

Penny: What I'm saying is people who get this information might start thinking they're experts – that they're qualified to make calls on things they don't really understand.

Penny is philosophical.

Edward: Well, that's not really what it's about. The idea is just to give an overview, guidelines, so that people will be able to flag potential problems, you know – they won't necessarily know how to deal with the problem, but they'll at least see there's a problem.

Edward is confused and frustrated.

Penny: Yes, I know, I was just saying...so you want my view on whether it gives a good, basic overview of the issues people need to be aware of?

Edward: Yes, exactly.

Edward is relieved and pleased.

Penny: In that case, you did a superb job. All the important information's there, but it's pitched at just the right level. *Penny is encouraging.*

Edward: That's what I was aiming for. Do you see anywhere I could improve it?

Edward is appreciative.

Penny: Perhaps. The only downside is that it's a little theoretical, a little abstract.

Penny is thoughtful.

Edward: So it would be hard for people who aren't familiar with compliance to really understand it?

Edward is thoughtful.

Penny: That could be a problem, yes. Sometimes things that are complex are easier to understand when you see them in action...

Edward: Right. Maybe if I included some examples...applied the theory to a practical scenario people could relate to.

Penny: Yes. And I think that approach would be helpful for you, too.

Edward: Oh? How so? *Edward is interested.*

Penny: You mentioned before that you found it difficult to see where concepts applied to "real life." Applying what you're learning to examples would clarify things.

Penny is helpful.

Edward: That's really helpful. Thanks! *Edward is appreciative.*

In giving feedback, Penny's performance was mixed. She didn't follow Edward's agenda, as her feedback didn't directly relate to his concern – instead she tried to divert the issue. However, she checked for understanding by confirming what he wanted. In her suggestion for improvement, Penny gave practical feedback. She also made a connection by explaining how using examples would clarify things for Edward and help him understand the material he's learning.

In giving feedback, Penny's performance was mixed. She didn't follow Edward's agenda, as her feedback didn't directly relate to his concern – instead she tried to divert the issue. However, she checked for understanding by confirming what he wanted. In her suggestion for improvement, Penny gave practical feedback. She also made a connection by explaining how using examples would clarify things for Edward and help him understand the material he's learning.

Case Study: Question 1 of 2

Scenario

For your convenience, the case study is repeated with each question.
Taku's a new employee at a residential real estate company. He
doesn't have much experience in selling, and feels his sales technique is holding him back. He raises this concern during a mentoring session with Celeste, his mentor. Follow along as Celeste
gives feedback to Taku.

Celeste: So you said in your e-mail you haven't met your targets
this month. How do you feel about that?
Celeste is calm.

Taku: Frustrated. I know I'm doing a lot of things right – I've
established good rapport with the vendors, I've arranged a lot
of viewings, attendance is good, and people are interested....but
they're just not buying...

Celeste: Ahh! I know! That's people for you! They're all talk, talk,
talk and then nothing. It's just like my brother-in-law. A couple
of months ago... *Celeste is animated.*

Taku: Your brother-in-law? He's interested in buying a house?
Taku is confused and frustrated.

Celeste: A house? Not that I know...no, what I meant was... *Celeste is confused.*

Taku: Actually, Celeste, I was hoping to talk about my approach
to selling, my technique...I'm not sure I'm going about it right –
you know, the way I talk to prospective purchasers...I kind of...
freeze when it comes to the crunch.
Taku is frustrated and impatient.

Celeste: OK, just so I understand...do you mean you lose confidence or you just don't know what to say to close a deal?
Celeste is interested.

Taku: It's that I don't know what to say...I don't want to appear
too pushy, but, at the same time, I know I need to get a commitment, move things along. It's about finding the balance between
the two.
Taku is disappointed and resigned.

Celeste: Well, it's difficult to know what to say...I'm not sure
what to tell you – it all depends on the particular situation, you
know. You need to read between the lines, get a sense of which

way the wind is blowing...you know?

Celeste is casual.

Taku: Well...I guess. It's all easier said than done, though. *Taku is cynical.*

Celeste: That's for sure! But listen, look at it this way – I know it's frustrating at first, but this is part of the learning curve. It's by having
these experiences that you'll improve. We've all gone through this. **Taku:** Well, that's reassuring, I suppose.

Taku is positive.

Question

Which statements about how Celeste provided feedback to Taku are true?

Options:

1. She followed his agenda by directly addressing his concerns about converting interest into sales
2. In addressing his doubts about the effectiveness of his sales approach, Celeste gave Taku feedback that he could act on
3. She checked for understanding by clarifying the specific reasons for his failure to close sales
4. Celeste helped Taku to see his current learning experience as movement forward toward his ultimate aim of being a better salesman

Answer

Option 1: *This option is incorrect. Instead of following Taku's agenda, Celeste diverted the issue by focusing instead on her views on human nature.*

Option 2: *This option is incorrect. Although a mentor should give feedback that the mentee can act on in a real way, Celeste didn't offer any concrete advice to Taku.*

Option 3: *This option is correct. Part of checking for understanding is to clarify what the mentee's saying, which Celeste did.*

Option 4: *This option is correct. Feedback should make a connection between learning and the mentoring journey. Celeste did this by explaining how Taku's challenges would aid his learning.*

Case Study: Question 2 of 2

Scenario

For your convenience, the case study is repeated with each question.
Taku's a new employee at a residential real estate company. He doesn't have much experience in selling, and feels his sales technique is holding him back. He raises this concern during a mentoring session with Celeste, his mentor. Follow along as Celeste gives feedback to Taku.

Celeste: So you said in your e-mail you haven't met your targets this month. How do you feel about that?

Celeste is calm.

Taku: Frustrated. I know I'm doing a lot of things right – I've established good rapport with the vendors, I've arranged a lot of viewings, attendance is good, and people are interested....but they're just not buying...

Celeste: Ahh! I know! That's people for you! They're all talk, talk, talk and then nothing. It's just like my brother-in-law. A couple of months ago... *Celeste is animated.*

Taku: Your brother-in-law? He's interested in buying a house? *Taku is confused and frustrated.*

Celeste: A house? Not that I know...no, what I meant was... *Celeste is confused.*

Taku: Actually, Celeste, I was hoping to talk about my approach to selling, my technique...I'm not sure I'm going about it right – you know, the way I talk to prospective purchasers...I kind of... freeze when it comes to the crunch.

Taku is frustrated and impatient.

Celeste: OK, just so I understand...do you mean you lose confidence or you just don't know what to say to close a deal?

Celeste is interested.

Taku: It's that I don't know what to say...I don't want to appear too pushy, but, at the same time, I know I need to get a commitment, move things along. It's about finding the balance between the two.

Taku is disappointed and resigned.

Celeste: Well, it's difficult to know what to say...I'm not sure what to tell you – it all depends on the particular situation, you know. You need to read between the lines, get a sense of which way the wind is blowing...you know?
Celeste is casual.
Taku: Well...I guess. It's all easier said than done, though. *Taku is cynical.*
Celeste: That's for sure! But listen, look at it this way – I know it's frustrating at first, but this is part of the learning curve. It's by having these experiences that you'll improve. We've all gone through this.
Taku: Well, that's reassuring, I suppose. *Taku is positive.*
Question
How could Celeste have provided better feedback to Taku?
Options:
1. She could have focused more directly on the techniques being used by Taku when trying to close a sale
2. She could have suggested tips on dealing with prospective clients or referred Taku to someone who could teach him effective sales techniques
3. She could have shown more compassion, sympathizing with Taku over this unfortunate interruption to his learning and progress
4. She could have made more effort to clearly understand Taku's problem

Answer
Option 1: This option is correct. Effective feedback is directly relevant and applicable to the mentee's concern, which, in Taku's case, is his inability to close sales.
Option 2: This option is correct. A mentor should give feedback that the mentee can respond to in a real way. Celeste could have helped Taku acquire the necessary skills.
Option 3: This option is incorrect. This wouldn't have been effective feedback, which should always indicate progress toward the ultimate goal.
Option 4: This option is incorrect. To be sure she understood the

issue, Celeste asked Taku whether his problem was psychological or practical.

Summary
To effectively manage a mentoring relationship, a mentor must allow the mentee to drive the relationship, ensure program awareness, help the mentee build a network of contacts, and keep records of issues discussed during sessions.

When giving feedback, mentors should follow the mentee's agenda, give practical feedback, check for understanding, and make a connection between learning and the bigger picture.

Mentees should be advised to make regular and specific requests for feedback, and to avoid reacting defensively to feedback.

KEEPING THE MENTORING PROGRAM ON TRACK

Guidelines for mentors

Mentoring relationships, like any other, aren't immune to problems. Issues can arise when there's too much – or too little – formality. Or an otherwise good mentoring relationship may suffer because of inadequate follow-up. There may be insufficient support within the organization for the mentoring program. Problems can also be a result of incompatibility between mentor and mentee, or interference from outside the relationship.

Consider this example of a mentoring relationship that's not working as intended. Stan, a long-standing employee at an advertising agency, is acting as mentor to Bill, a new employee. Follow along as Stan and Bill begin one of their weekly mentoring sessions.

Stan: Hey, how are you? Listen, could we make this quick? I'm kind of busy today.

Stan is impatient and distracted.

Bill: Um, yeah...it's just the mentoring session really. We have one scheduled for now.

Bill is hesitant and insulted.

Stan: Oh, OK. So...you need some more "mentoring," do you?

Stan is disinterested.

Bill: Well, from the schedule that HR sent me, we have a session scheduled for today...

Bill is offended.

Stan: OK. So what's the problem? Do you have some questions?

Bill: Actually, not really. I was just told to come and see you at 11 today. So I came. I don't really know what this is all supposed to be about.

Bill is irritated.

Stan: OK. Great, then. No problems, no questions. I'll write that down. See you next week, I suppose. Same time, is it?

Stan is pleased.

Bill: Yes, it is. Same time, same day, every week.... *Bill is irritated.*

Stan: Just one thing, before you go. Are you finding this helpful? This mentoring thing?

Stan is oblivious.

Bill: Oh sure. It's a lot of help. I don't think I could manage without it.

Bill is sarcastic.

Stan: Super! That's great to hear. *Stan is pleased.*

What did you think of this mentoring relationship? Stan doesn't seem to have any interest in being a mentor or in his mentee. And there clearly isn't much support within the organization for the program. The HR Department told Bill to attend a mentoring session, but didn't give him any information on what to expect or what to prepare. For Bill, the entire experience is a waste of time.

During the course of a mentoring relationship, mentors will inevitably encounter problems and challenges. Some of these will relate to the purpose of the relationship, but others will stem from personal, professional, or technical issues.

Reflect

What do you think a mentor could do to ensure problems don't get out of hand?

In thinking about what a mentor could do, you perhaps thought of making sure to set boundaries and expectations at the outset so that everyone knows what is and isn't part of the relationship. It's also advisable to stay away from a mentee's personal issues unless they're impacting the relationship. A mentor should also avoid trying to solve every problem for the mentee. This is counterproductive and usually impossible.

For example, setting boundaries and expectations could mean a mentor makes it clear from the outset what can and can't be included in a mentoring session. Inappropriate issues could be things such as the mentee's employment contract status or vacation entitlements.

Avoiding personal issues could mean a mentor draws the line at any discussion of, for example, the mentee's marital difficulties. A mentor shouldn't try to provide a solution to everything because this could lead to the mentee becoming dependent on the mentor. For instance, a mentor could offer guidance, advice, and feedback, but shouldn't actually do the mentee's work.

2. Preventing program issues

Problems with mentoring programs tend to be either procedural or contextual. Procedural problems relate to how the mentoring program is managed. Overmanagement stifles spontaneity, while undermanagement drains momentum. Contextual problems relate to clarity of purpose or the support given to the mentoring program within the organization. Clarity of purpose means everyone knows why something's being done, what's expected, what the aim is, and who's responsible for what. A lack of support from senior management undermines and diminishes a mentoring program.

Problems affecting the mentoring program can be prevented by careful planning and design. There are five key guidelines for preventing program issues, whether procedural or contextual. These are to select and match mentors and mentees effectively, provide training to prepare participants for their roles, plan for mentoring, provide support for participants, and avoid excessive bureaucracy. Most program-related problems are avoidable if there's good planning and design during the initial stages.

See each guideline to find out more about it.

Select and match effectively

Selecting and matching mentors and mentees effectively requires a clear idea about what constitutes a good mentor and a good mentee.

A good mentor has a positive attitude toward mentoring, can assist others, and possesses the required experience and expertise. A good mentee matches the program's target group, and is keen and able to participate.

Nobody should be forced to participate – coercion affects motivation, resulting in apathy at best, and disruption at worst.

Provide training

Providing training helps participants to quickly adjust to the often unfamiliar requirements of mentoring. It helps them understand their roles, gives them the required skills, and introduces them to guidelines on managing the relationship.

It's also a good idea to provide training to individuals, such as line managers, who aren't directly involved in the mentoring program. This prevents misunderstandings about their roles and the mentor's role, which, if unaddressed, could lead to resentment toward the mentor or interference in the relationship.

Plan for mentoring

Effectively planning the mentoring program means devoting time and resources to determining whether there's a real need for the program, its goals, the level of support for the program, whether it'll be welcomed by participants, and how its performance will be measured. It also means setting objectives and measuring results.

Select and match effectively

Selecting and matching mentors and mentees effectively requires a clear idea about what constitutes a good mentor and a good mentee.

A good mentor has a positive attitude toward mentoring, can assist others, and possesses the required experience and expertise. A good mentee matches the program's target group, and is keen and able to participate.

Nobody should be forced to participate – coercion affects motivation, resulting in apathy at best, and disruption at worst.

Provide training

Providing training helps participants to quickly adjust to the often unfamiliar requirements of mentoring. It helps them understand their roles, gives them the required skills, and introduces them to guidelines on managing the relationship.

It's also a good idea to provide training to individuals, such as line managers, who aren't directly involved in the mentoring program. This prevents misunderstandings about their roles and the mentor's role, which, if unaddressed, could lead to resentment toward the mentor or interference in the relationship.

Plan for mentoring

Effectively planning the mentoring program means devoting time and resources to determining whether there's a real need for the program, its goals, the level of support for the program, whether it'll be welcomed by participants, and how its performance will be measured. It also means setting objectives and measuring results.

Accurately defining the program's ultimate and interim goals helps participants understand the reasons for the program, which can motivate them to participate fully.

It's also necessary to establish the criteria for measuring success. This shows whether relationships are functioning and on track, and whether the program is operating as intended.

Provide support

In addition to the initial training, it's important to provide ongoing support to those participating in the mentoring program. This is essential to safeguard against participants feeling isolated, facilitate further development, and build effective relationships.

Support could be in the form of workshops or review meetings, perhaps facilitated by the program coordinator. Another option would be to make learning resources – such as books, jour-nals, online material, or conference attendance – available to participants.

Avoid excessive bureaucracy

It's critical to avoid excessive bureaucracy in a mentoring pro-gram. The challenge is to achieve the right balance between formality and informality, because some formality is neces-sary. There needs to be enough formality to build a supportive network, yet enough informality to allow the relationship to develop in line with the participants' needs and wants.

When striking the balance between formality and informality, it's useful to remember that a mentoring relationship is a liv-ing relationship. As it evolves and progresses, so too should the rules and policies.

For example, Abu is coordinating a mentoring program for Man-uel, a new employee in his company's Accounts Department. Abu discusses the options with Manuel, who immediately re-quests Dawn as his mentor. However, Abu knows that Dawn doesn't have a lot of spare time and can be abrupt with new employees. Abu suggests Betty, who has an excellent under-standing of account procedures, and is very welcoming to new staff. Betty is also an enthusiastic advocate of mentoring. This is effective matching.

The program has a clear purpose – to ease Manuel's transition into his new role. To facilitate this, Betty is to be a point of con-tact for queries, a source of feedback on projects he's working on, and a sounding board for his ideas.

Abu organizes an orientation and training session for Manuel and Betty. This is to ensure they clearly understand what "being a mentor" and "being a mentee" is all about. Manuel learns that it's his responsibility to drive the agenda. Betty learns the im-portance of allowing Manuel to do this, and not trying to take control of the relationship.

Abu also ensures there's support for the relationship. He gets approval from Manuel and Betty's direct manager that they can spend an hour each week on the relationship. He also arranges for the Accounts Department's internal guidelines to be collated within a single resource for Manuel's convenience. Abu makes himself available for monthly review meetings.

Although Abu knows that some formality and bureaucracy can be helpful to give structure to the program, he's careful to avoid burdening either Manuel or Betty. He feels the monthly review meetings will be sufficient to keep the relationship on track, so he doesn't ask anything else of them.

Case Study: Question 1 of 2

Scenario

For your convenience, the case study is repeated with each question.

Hannah, an HR manager, is disappointed that a mentoring relationship she coordinated is struggling after just three months.

Both Richard, a senior manager and the mentor, and Dorothy, a new employee and the mentee, were initially very enthusiastic about the program. Dorothy specifically requested Richard as her mentor, as he has the skills she wants to learn. And Richard was keen to mentor Dorothy because he sees potential in her.

Hannah arranged training provided by a mentoring program consultant who explained the participants' respective roles and introduced them to guidelines on conducting mentoring relationships.

Assess how this mentoring program could have been better managed and coordinated, and then answer the questions in order.

Question

Hannah's confused and frustrated because, as far as she can tell, she did everything right. However Dorothy now describes the experience as "a waste of time" and "pointless," while Richard says he has "no idea" what the program's supposed to achieve. Richard also says he feels the program "exists within a vacuum with no contact or interaction with the outside world." What's worse, he's unhappy that he wasn't previously told there would be "so much unnecessary paperwork," which, he says, he doesn't

107

have time for.

What should Hannah have done to avoid the problems that arose in the mentoring relationship?

Options:

1. She should have thought more about who'd be a good mentor for Dorothy, because Richard was clearly a poor choice
2. She should have arranged more effective training as it's obvious that Richard and Dorothy don't understand how a mentoring relationship works
3. She should have paid more attention to determining the overall aim of the program, and this should have been clearly communicated to the participants
4. She should have provided adequate ongoing support to the relationship, something she and the organization failed to do

5. She should have avoided making excessive bureaucratic and administrative demands on the participants

Answer

Option 1: This option is incorrect. It's important to effectively select and match mentors and mentees, but Dorothy and Richard were a good match. Both had a positive attitude toward participation.

Option 2: This option is incorrect. Hannah organized training for Richard and Dorothy to ensure both understood their respective roles and guidelines on conducting mentoring relationships.

Option 3: This option is correct. Effectively planning a mentoring program requires that the objectives of the program are clearly defined and communicated. Neither Dorothy nor Richard had a clear understanding of the program's aims.

Option 4: This option is correct. It's important to provide ongoing support to those participating in a mentoring program so participants don't feel isolated. However, it's clear that the mentoring relationship between Richard and Dorothy received no support from the organization.

Option 5: This option is correct. An effective relationship should

108

*be devoid of excessive bureaucracy. It's clear from Richard's com-
plaint about the volume of paperwork he was expected to fill out
that this mentoring program didn't meet this requirement.*

Case Study: Question 2 of 2
Scenario
For your convenience, the case study is repeated with each question.

Hannah, an HR manager, is disappointed that a mentoring relationship she coordinated is
struggling after just three months.
Both Richard, a senior manager and the mentor, and Dorothy, a new employee and the mentee, were initially very enthusiastic about the program. Dorothy specifically requested Richard as her mentor, as he has the skills she wants to learn. And Richard was keen to mentor Dorothy because he sees potential in her.
Hannah arranged training provided by a mentoring program consultant who explained the participants' respective roles and introduced them to guidelines on conducting mentoring relationships.
Assess how this mentoring program could have been better managed and coordinated, and then answer the questions in order.
Question
Aside from Hannah's mistakes, Richard made a number of errors in how he conducted himself as a mentor.
Which actions, taken by Richard during mentoring, were inappropriate?
Options:
1. During the first mentoring session, he told Dorothy to feel free to bring any issue, problem, question, or request to him, insisting there were no limits
2. On one occasion when Dorothy was having domestic problems, he offered to speak with her husband on her behalf so as to offer a male perspective

3. Early in the relationship, he explained to Dorothy that he could guide and advise her, but that it wouldn't be appropriate for him to try to solve her problems for her

4. He devoted one entire mentoring session to discussing her hopes and expectations for the relationship, and agreeing on what it would cover

Answer

Option 1: This option is correct. Richard should have set boundaries and expectations at the beginning of the relationship, ensuring Dorothy understood what issues and areas were covered.

Option 2: This option is correct. Unless a mentee's personal life is adversely affecting the relationship, it's advisable for mentors to avoid getting involved in personal matters.

Option 3: This option is incorrect. A mentor shouldn't try to solve every problem for the mentee. Richard was correct to take this position.

Option 4: This option is incorrect. It's important for a mentor to set boundaries and

expectations at the outset so that it's clear what is and isn't part of the relationship. Richard was correct to make this clear.

Summary

Problems and challenges will almost inevitably arise during any mentoring relationship.

To minimize problems, the mentor should set boundaries and expectations at the outset so everyone knows what is and isn't part of the relationship. The mentor should also avoid getting involved in the mentee's personal issues, and should avoid trying to solve every problem.

Key guidelines for ensuring there are no program-related problems are to select and match mentors and mentees effectively, provide training to prepare participants for their roles, plan for mentoring, provide support for participants, and avoid excessive bureaucracy.

ADDRESSING INTERPERSONAL ISSUES IN MENTORING

Importance of addressing problems

Although mentoring can be an enhancing experience for participants, it's not always easy. There can be problems from grievances, personality clashes, communication issues, or misinterpretations. To maintain and develop a mentoring relationship, you must address any interpersonal issues.

Reflect

Why do you think it's so important to deal with interpersonal problems in mentoring relationships?

In thinking about the importance of dealing with interpersonal problems, you perhaps thought of the need to maintain the integrity of the mentoring program. A program's integrity can be damaged by interpersonal problems, particularly if they're not addressed. Dealing with interpersonal problems also ensures the participants remain appreciative of each other. Respect and understanding are central to mentoring relationships. However, when there are interpersonal problems, participants often make unfavorable or unfair assessments of one another.

Consider, for example, the experience of Ellen and her mentor Pamela. Ellen is not comfortable with Pamela, suspecting she's motivated by self-interest and nothing else. She can't talk openly with Pamela. Pamela says Ellen is too serious and doesn't have the personality traits required for effective mentoring. Pamela has lost respect for Ellen.

The integrity of this relationship has been damaged. There's little prospect of there being respect, trust, or open communication, but these are critical qualities of an effective relationship. Without them, the relationship won't achieve its aims.

Also, Ellen and Pamela don't currently appreciate one another. Instead of respect and understanding, there's distrust, cynicism, and dislike. Each has identified negative and unappealing traits in the other.

Unlike problems to do with the design or implementation of the mentoring program, interpersonal problems can't always be avoided through good planning. There are some core interpersonal problems that can emerge during a mentoring relationship, including a failure to establish rapport, unrealistic expectations, a lack of commitment or time, dependency on the part of the mentee, and problems with others.

2. Failure to establish rapport

Failure to establish rapport is one problem that can impact a mentoring relationship. For there to be rapport, it helps if there's a clear purpose to the relationship. This provides a common point of interest and reference. Rapport grows when people work together toward a common goal. Participants must at least recognize the validity of each other's values. This doesn't mean mentors must share mentees' beliefs about what's important, but they should respect these beliefs.

Consider again the case of Ellen and Pamela. Right now, there's little rapport between the colleagues, and the prospects of developing trust or confidence aren't looking good. The problem stems from there being no clear or agreed purpose to the relationship and no recognition of the validity of one another's values.

See each characteristic of the relationship between Ellen and Pamela to find out how it's obstructing the development of rapport.

No clear or agreed purpose

Instead of a clear or agreed purpose, Ellen and Pamela each identify completely different purposes to their mentoring relationship.

Ellen's aim is to develop the skills and competencies required for her present job. But Pamela sees this as pointless. Pamela constantly tells Ellen that her present job is just a stopgap and not worth focusing on. According to Pamela, if Ellen wants to succeed, she should develop the qualities valued by the organization at its highest levels.

No recognition of validity

There's no recognition from either Ellen or Pamela of the validity of the other's values.

Ellen values attention to detail, careful analysis, and team orientation, while Pamela values competitiveness and decisiveness.

Pamela sees Ellen's values as signs of weakness, and tells her she'll never progress unless she relaxes her attitude. Ellen believes Pamela's values to be cynical and self-interested.

Can Ellen and Pamela rectify their problems? With the help of Ronald, the program coordinator, they work together to agree on the program's purpose, with both explaining clearly their hopes for the program. As a result, Ellen recognizes that she'd gain more from the program by focusing on her longer- term career development.

Ronald also helps them to acknowledge and respect the validity of each other's values, and Pamela comes to accept that her way isn't necessarily the only valid way. They go on to build a strong working relationship, accepting each other's personalities and focusing on each other's strong points toward meeting their goals.

However, in certain situations, it might not be possible – despite the best efforts of the mentor, mentee, and coordinator –

for participants to "agree to disagree" and develop rapport on this basis. The best solution then would be for everyone to accept this and move on by dissolving the relationship. The mentee is then free to find another mentor with whom there's compatibility and a real prospect of building rapport.

Question

In which situations would the development of rapport between mentor and mentee be obstructed?

Options:

1. Neither mentor nor mentee really understands what they're supposed to be working toward
2. The mentor dismisses the mentee's values as nonsensical and misinformed
3. Both participants have completely different views about what's important and how tasks should be approached
4. Although the purpose of the relationship has been made clear, the mentor believes the aims should be more ambitious

Answer

Option 1: *This option is correct. For there to be rapport, it helps if there's a clear purpose to the relationship, such as the mentee's development or career requirements.*

Option 2: *This option is correct. For rapport to develop, both mentor and mentee must at least recognize the validity of the other's values.*

Option 3: *This option is incorrect. Although it's important for participants to respect one another's values, it's not necessary for them to share common beliefs about what's important and how things should be done.*

Option 4: *This option is incorrect. As long as there's a clear purpose to the relationship so participants know what they're working toward, there can be rapport. It's not necessary that there be universal agreement.*

Unrealistic expectations

It's important that mentees don't have unrealistic expectations about what participation in the mentoring program means. This issue can be addressed through open and frank discussions, providing clarification on what can and can't be expected. These discussions should ideally take place early in the relationship.

Mentees should understand that the mentoring relationship won't meet all of their needs and solve all of their problems. They should also understand that it won't last forever or transform their careers.

It should also be understood that promotion isn't guaranteed as a result of participating in a mentoring program, even though it might enhance mentees' promotion prospects.

Failing to address unrealistic expectations may damage the relationship and cause resentment from both sides. The mentee may feel betrayed or let down, while the mentor may feel unappreciated.

Consider the example of Ernie and his mentor Arnold. One problem in this relationship is that Ernie has unrealistic expectations about what his participation in the mentoring program means.

In their first session, Ernie tells Arnold that he wants to learn everything there is to know about his current role. He expects Arnold to act as a hands-on tutor, teaching him every detail of the department's internal procedures.

However, Arnold doesn't see this as his responsibility. Arnold understands that his role will be to provide guidance, advice, and feedback. Ernie feels let down by Arnold.

To help Ernie form more realistic expectations, Libby, the program coordinator, intervenes. With both participants speaking frankly and openly, they succeed in clarifying what Ernie can realistically and reasonably expect from the relationship. Ernie now understands and accepts that it's unrealistic to expect Arnold to invest the amount of time required to do all the things he had wanted.

Question

What would be effective ways of dealing with a mentee's unrealistic expectations?

Options:

1. Provide clarification on what can and can't be expected
2. Explain that a mentoring program can't possibly meet every need or solve every problem
3. Assign the mentee to a different mentor who's able and prepared to meet these expectations
4. Remind the mentor of the need to do whatever it takes to facilitate the mentee's development

Answer

Option 1: This option is correct. The best way to deal with unrealistic expectations is through an open, frank discussion about what can be expected.

Option 2: This option is correct. It's important for mentees to understand and accept that a mentoring program cannot solve every problem or meet every need. Belief in the contrary is often at the root of unrealistic expectations.

Option 3: This option is incorrect. When a mentee's expectations are unrealistic, the choice of mentor has nothing to do with problems encountered in the mentoring relationship.

Option 4: This option is incorrect. It's impossible to provide everything a mentee might want. If expectations are unrealistic, they can't be met.

Lack of commitment or time

A lack of commitment or time is among the most common problems that affect mentoring relationships. People with the most to offer as mentors – those with experience and expertise – tend to be busy and short on time. Mentors who are busy sometimes give the mentoring program low priority. When mentors are under pressure with other responsibilities, it's often the mentee who loses out.

The best way to address this problem is to emphasize the importance of mentoring within the organization. This could be done by setting aside time in the mentor's schedule for the mentoring relationship. Or the mentoring program coordinator could actively monitor session times and frequencies, making it more likely that the mentor will prioritize mentoring.

It's also helpful for participants to openly discuss time constraints and find a solution. If face-to-face sessions aren't always possible, phone calls or e-mail communication may be suitable alternatives.

A mentor who resents having to attend mentoring sessions or who regularly misses appointments might not be a suitable mentor.

This was a problem that affected the mentoring relationship between a mentee, Esther, and her mentor Vicky. Esther complained to Bart, the program coordinator, about Vicky's repeated failure to turn up for scheduled mentoring sessions.

Vicky responded, saying that because of her workload, and because she was required to travel regularly on business, it was impossible for her to attend every scheduled session.

After discussing the options with Esther and Vicky, Bart drafts a new schedule. Esther and Vicky will meet face-to-face whenever possible, but will conduct their mentoring sessions by phone whenever.

Vicky is away.

Question

Which solutions would work in a situation where the mentor lacks commitment or time?

Options:

1. Emphasize how highly the organization values mentoring
2. Ensure the mentor schedules enough time for mentoring
3. Threaten the mentor with disciplinary action unless mentoring responsibilities are prioritized

4. Explain to the mentee that a mentoring program can't meet every need

Answer

Option 1: *This option is correct. The best way to address a lack of commitment is to make it clear that the organization places immense value on mentoring.*

Option 2: *This option is correct. Setting aside time for mentoring responsibilities protects the schedule from being compromised by other demands.*

Option 3: *This option is incorrect. A mentor who clearly lacks commitment isn't a suitable mentor, and coercion won't change this.*

Option 4: *This option is incorrect. While unrealistic expectations need to be dealt with, lack of commitment on the part of the mentor needs to be addressed.*

Mentee becomes dependent

Although mentoring should foster independence, competence, and self-drive, some mentees become dependent on their mentors. Dependency is unhealthy for both parties. Mentees must take responsibility for their own development, and not look to mentors to be responsible. When mentees are given practice, feedback, and formal intervention, they become more confident in their abilities and capacity to drive their own development. Part of a mentor's role is to enable and encourage a mentee's independence.

Recall the example of Ellen and Pamela. There was a problem of dependency in the relationship between Ellen and Pamela. While Ellen knew what she wanted from the mentoring program, she seemed to believe that it was Pamela's job to achieve these things on her behalf. She transferred responsibility for her development to Pamela.

Early in the relationship, she asked Pamela to "teach me everything I need to know." Pamela explained that her role was to assist Ellen's own learning and development with guidance and feedback.

To address this problem, Pamela suggested tasks to Ellen,

guided her approach to these tasks, and gave feedback on the results. Gradually, Ellen became more confident and assured in her ability to drive her own development – and less dependent on Pamela.

Question

Which approaches would be effective ways of dealing with dependency?

Options:

1. The mentor works with the mentee to encourage greater responsibility and independence
2. The mentor provides constructive feedback to build the mentee's confidence and self-belief
3. The mentor temporarily assumes responsibility for the mentee's development until the mentee is more able
4. The mentee is immediately ejected from the mentoring program to force independent behavior

Answer

Option 1: *This option is correct. Because dependency is unhealthy for the mentee, the mentor should work to enable and encourage independence.*

Option 2: *This option is correct. When mentees are given constructive feedback, they become more confident in their abilities and capacity to drive their own development.*

Option 3: *This option is incorrect. Any form of dependence is unhealthy for the mentee and the mentor, and shouldn't be facilitated.*

Option 4: *This option is incorrect. Although it's important to address dependence, ejection from the program could be counterproductive.*

Problems with others

Problems with other people – people who aren't part of the mentoring relationship – can also cause difficulties in the relationship. These problems generally involve either the mentee's colleagues or direct manager.

See each of the potential sources of problems to find out more about it.

Colleagues

There may be problems with the mentee's colleagues, especially when the purpose of the mentoring program isn't clear.

Problems with other employees often stem from jealousy or resentment. There might be a belief that the mentee is being treated favorably or groomed for promotion ahead of others.

These problems can be dealt with through transparency and openness about the program. If there's a lack of transparency or a perception of secrecy, there's more likely to be gossip and idle speculation.

It's also a good idea to publicize the inclusion criteria – explain why some employees have been included and others have not.

Direct manager

A mentee's direct manager may feel threatened by the mentoring relationship. This could be due to suspicions about what's going on and being said within the mentoring sessions.

There may also be resentment if it's felt that the mentee is prioritizing mentoring program responsibilities over actual job responsibilities. Direct managers might feel it's their job to mentor and develop their direct reports, and may resent outside involvement.

This is why it's important to involve the mentee's manager as much as possible, or to at least ensure that there's complete openness about the relationship.

Now consider the experience of Sam, a mentee, and Gabriel, his mentor. When it became known within Sam's department that he was being mentored by Gabriel, an executive in the organization, the reaction was negative. No other employee had ever been given a mentor as senior as Gabriel. This led to speculation that Sam – despite being the youngest and least experienced employee in the department – was being prepared for a managerial position. This caused hostility toward him.

Sam's manager also reacted badly. He was angry that, without any explanation, responsibility for developing one of his employees had been taken away from him. He was suspicious about the reasons for this.

To address these problems, Martha, the program coordinator, explains the relationship's purpose. She says that Gabriel was chosen as mentor because of his unique skills and experience. She also explains to Sam's manager that senior management felt he had too many other responsibilities, and that it would have been unfair to ask him to take on the job of mentoring Sam.

Question

What would be appropriate ways of dealing with problems with a mentee's direct manager or colleagues?

Options:

1. Explain that the mentee isn't being given preferential treatment, but may benefit developmentally from mentoring more than other employees
2. Give the mentee's direct manager a role in the mentoring program, perhaps assisting the mentor in guiding the mentee's development
3. Publicly state that all those with a problem should reflect on their level of professionalism and personal maturity
4. Respect the confidentiality of the mentoring relationship's participants, and explain that it's inappropriate to comment on speculation

Answer

Option 1: *This option is correct. It's important that a mentee's colleagues understand why the mentee was selected for mentoring when others weren't. This reduces the likelihood that others will become jealous.*

Option 2: *This option is correct. The mentee's manager should be as involved as possible, as this makes it less likely that the relationship will be regarded as a threat.*

Option 3: *This option is incorrect. Problems involving other people should be addressed by being transparent and open about the pro-*

gram. Criticizing the negative reactions of others wouldn't help the situation.

Option 4: *This option is incorrect. Although certain aspects of a mentoring relationship should be confidential, its purpose and the criteria used to select participants should be open and transparent.*

Question

You need to resolve a number of interpersonal problems that are affecting the mentoring relationship between Consuela, the mentor, and Sumie, the mentee.

Match the interpersonal problems that are affecting the relationship to possible solutions.

Options:

A. Consuela doesn't feel there's any "connection" between herself and Sumie

B. Sumie asks what her new job title will be after completing the mentoring program C. Sumie is unhappy that Consuela often misses scheduled mentoring sessions

D. Sumie doesn't think that Consuela is doing enough to advance her career

E. Sumie's colleagues have been unfriendly since the mentoring program began

Targets:

1. Establish rapport by working together to revise and agree on the purpose of the relationship
2. Clarify that participation in the program won't necessarily lead to immediate promotion
3. Announce that, as coordinator, you'll be monitoring session times and frequencies
4. Suggest that Consuela give Sumie more feedback on her performance to build confidence
5. Make it known that Sumie was selected for the mentoring program because of her inexperience

Answer

Ensuring agreement on the purpose of the relationship is an appropriate solution to a lack of "connection" or rapport between partici-

pants. For there to be rapport, it helps if there's a clear and agreed purpose.

Clarifying what can and cannot be expected is an appropriate solution to unrealistic expectations. It's important to ensure that Sumie doesn't have unrealistic expectations about what participating in the program will mean for her.

Careful monitoring is an appropriate solution to a lack of commitment from the mentor. Consuela will be more likely to prioritize her mentoring responsibilities when she knows her commitment is being monitored.

Providing confidence-building feedback is an appropriate solution to the mentee becoming

dependent on the mentor. Feedback would boost Sumie's confidence in her own ability and her capacity to drive her own development.

Openly explaining the selection criteria is an appropriate solution to problems with others. Sumie's colleagues appear to be jealous about her selection, perhaps seeing it as favorable treatment. The best way to deal with this is through transparency and openness about the program.

Summary

It's important to directly address any interpersonal issues that arise in a mentoring relationship. This maintains the integrity of the mentoring program and ensures that participants remain appreciative of each other.

There are several interpersonal problems that can emerge during a mentoring relationship. There could be a failure to establish rapport, which may mean the relationship needs to be dissolved. It's also a problem if the mentee has unrealistic expectations of the relationship, so it's important to clarify expectations at the outset. A lack of commitment or time is a common problem which can be addressed by emphasizing the importance of mentoring and personnel development.

Another problem is mentee dependency on the mentor. There can also be problems with others outside the relationship, such as a mentee's direct manager or colleagues. Such problems can generally be overcome by ensuring there's complete openness about the relationship.

ESSENTIAL MENTORING TECHNIQUES: EVALUATING AND ENDING THE MENTORING PROGRAM

Mentoring programs can be of huge value to your organization. But how can you know they are really working? While many decision makers instinctively know that mentoring is of benefit, instinct is not enough. If the mentoring programs aren't evaluated, CEOs and board members have no way of knowing whether the investment of resources is paying off. When this happens, programs often lose their momentum and either fail or are terminated completely.

The purpose of evaluation is to assess whether the program is achieving the objectives it has set, and whether it should be continued or altered. Because programs require a lot of time and investment, it's essential that they be assessed. Assessing progress against defined objectives, during its course and at the end, is key to maintaining a successful mentoring program.

The relationships between mentors and mentees are critical to the success of the program. These relationships need to be assessed and managed correctly. Mentors need to assess their own mentoring skills in order to maintain quality relationships. They also need to know how to end the relationship professionally. It's important that mentors and mentees agree on the criteria for how the program will end, whether it's ending prematurely or reaching its natural end.

This course outlines how mentors can use self-assessments to improve their mentoring skills and enhance their relationships. It then describes appropriate methods program coordinators can use to assess the success of their organization's mentoring program. Finally, the course discusses guidelines and strategies for ending mentoring relationships professionally.

MENTORING SELF-ASSESSMENT

What to assess

How can an organization know that the time and resources it puts into a mentoring program are worth it? When designing a mentoring program, you need to carefully consider the benefits you hope to achieve from it. Then in order to measure whether the program has achieved these benefits, you must put in place appropriate measurement and evaluation processes.

The best way to assess a mentoring program's effectiveness is to measure it on an ongoing basis – this is known as formative evaluation. It's also important to assess your program at the end, or after important milestones are reached – give it what's called a summative evaluation. To understand the difference between formative and summative evaluation, think of formative as smaller, ongoing measurements and summative as more formal, final measurements. Self-assessments are used regularly to provide formative evaluations of mentors' performance.

Reflect

Before a mentor can be evaluated, it's important to understand what makes a good mentor. What skills do you think are necessary to be a successful mentor?

You may have noted a number of key interpersonal skills that mentors should have. Mentors may possess some of these naturally, and others can be built upon and honed over time:

- First, effective mentors listen carefully to their mentees and ask appropriate questions to check how they're feeling about the process and their own progress.

- They also give meaningful feedback – that is, honest feedback about what their mentees do well and what needs improvement. Mentors aim to provide constructive feedback that links achievements to the outcomes the mentor and mentee have set together.

- Mentors also set goals and expectations that are agreed on by both parties as being appropriate to the mentees' current stage of development. They guide and challenge mentees to move forward in achieving their overall objectives.

- Effective mentors focus on relationship building to create an atmosphere where mentees feel supported and understood but don't become dependent. They are accessible to their mentees.

- When necessary, good mentors employ a variety of problem-solving and conflict-resolution techniques in order to maintain positive relationships. They'll be open to creative solutions to problems or disagreements that suit each situation. Analytical thinking comes into play here as well – this helps the mentor to be objective and find the best solution.

- A good mentor incorporates advocacy into the mentoring style. This could involve seeking to promote or praise mentees to others, inspiring mentees and encouraging them to believe in their potential, and helping them to build up their own network of contacts whenever possible.

You can create your own self-assessment questionnaire to develop your mentoring skills and monitor improvement over time. Select each of the skills for examples of the type of questions you can use.

Listen and ask questions
To assess your listening skills, you can ask yourself these questions:
- Do I look people in the eye when I'm speaking with them?

- Do I listen carefully to what they're saying and ask relevant questions to show that I'm listening?

Give meaningful feedback

To improve on how you give feedback, ask yourself questions like these:

- Do I seek to provide meaningful feedback in a constructive and nonjudgmental manner? - Am I open to feedback on my own feedback methods?

- Do I try to give feedback as timely as possible following an event?

Set goals and expectations

A key part of being a good listener is helping mentees to set goals and expectations. To assess whether you're setting appropriate **SMART** goals ask yourself whether the goals you set with the mentee are

Specific

Measurable

Achievable

Realistic, and

Time-bound.

Relationship building

If you're to be successful as a mentor, you also need to have good relationship building skills. Ask yourself questions like these:

- Do I offer support and encouragement without creating dependency? - Do I create an atmosphere of continuous development?

- Do I exemplify integrity by following through on my commitments?

Problem solving and conflict resolution

Throughout the course of the relationship, problems and conflict will inevitably arise at some point. To assess how well you handle problems and conflict, ask yourself questions like these:

- Am I open to considering more than one cause and solution to a problem?

- Do I ask probing questions to try to get to the root of an issue?

- Do I seek to gather information from a variety of sources when

resolving a dispute?
- Do I take the context of a situation into account when making decisions?
- Do I try to identify the best possible route to take to minimize cost and maximize benefits?

Advocacy

To be an advocate to your mentees, ask yourself questions like these:
- When was the last time I spoke highly of my mentees or introduced them to a useful contact?
- Do I encourage my mentees to really apply what they are learning and take action so that they understand the value of their efforts?

Question
Match each mentor skill to a question mentors might ask themselves in self-assessment

Options:

A. Listen and ask questions
B. Problem solving and conflict resolution C. Advocacy
D. Relationship building
E. Set goals and expectations
F. Give meaningful feedback

Targets:

1. "Are my questions relevant to what my mentees are saying?"
2. "Do I gather as much information as possible before making conclusions?"
3. "How can I encourage my mentees to believe in their potential?"
4. "Do I try to be as supportive as possible without encouraging dependency?"
5. "Do I establish realistic outcomes with my mentee?"
6. "Do I give constructive criticism that helps my mentees perform better?"

Answer

It's important to show that you're really listening to your mentees by asking relevant questions.

To maintain a healthy relationship you need to be able to resolve conflict through analytical, objective thinking.

It's important to be an advocate to your mentee. This can mean praising mentees to others.

To build good relationships, mentees benefit from support but also from independence.

Encouraging mentees to set realistic goals will help to increase motivation.

Mentors aim to provide constructive feedback that links achievements to the objectives that were set.

Setting self-improvement goals

No matter how skilled a mentor you are, a mentoring relationship will need time to settle and develop naturally, while both participants acclimatize to each other. Monitoring helps demonstrate how the relationship is growing and evolving over time. Mentor self-assessments are one of the most effective ways to ensure a mentoring program works effectively. It's important that mentors and mentees regularly review what's happening. They should discuss their mentoring meetings, the relationship, and what's being learned regularly.

Self-assessment of your mentoring skills enables you to see how well you're performing as a mentor. A large part of the learning curve for the mentor occurs in closing the gap between where the mentee is now and at different stages of the process.

Self-assessments help mentors to select which path is best for them. They help to enhance mentoring relationships as mentors become more adept at empathizing with their mentees and more aware of themselves and their own skill level.

Self-assessment on its own is not enough. Mentors and mentees should meet regularly to assess the relationship using results of the self assessment. From there, they can review strengths and weaknesses of the relationship.

By discussing your relationship, often you get a better feel for how you're both progressing. The results of your self-assessment should be linked directly to your mentoring strategy. First, use the results to set goals for self-improvement. From this you can create a mentoring development plan. Finally, you can start to encourage improvement through action.

The first step you can take is to explore how to set appropriate goals for self-improvement. To do this, try to identify ways you can enhance mentoring skills.

Question
Which statement about setting goals to improve your mentoring skills do you think is true?

Options:
1. You should use your answers from mentoring self-assessments to help you identify goals and expectations
2. You should try to identify goals and expectations for improvement while you are carrying out self-assessments
3. Goals and expectations don't necessarily relate to your self-assessments

Answer

Option 1: *This is the correct option. By analyzing your answers to questions about the different mentoring skills, you can identify what goals you want to achieve in order to improve.*

Option 2: *This option is incorrect. The answers from your self-assessments help you to then form your goals and expectations for improvement.*

Option 3: *This option is incorrect. The self-assessment results inform you of which of the mentoring skills you need improvement in, and it's from this feedback that you identify goals for improvement.*

Self-assessments provide the basis for developing your goals and expectations. Linking your areas of weakness to your goals is the key to a practical plan for improvement.

For example, if the results of your self-assessment show that you need to work on developing better listening skills, you need to identify ways to enhance this skill. You might decide to keep a journal about certain interactions you felt were positive or negative and reflect on them in order to improve.

Developing listening skills then becomes one of your goals for self-improvement and the journal is part of your plan to enhance this skill.

Consider this example. A mentor, Alan, has completed his self-assessment on the five mentor skills and is now identifying his goals for improvement.

Alan assesses his responses and identifies that he needs to improve his relationship building skills. As a result, he sets a goal for himself: to follow through on commitments in a timely manner.

Creating a mentoring plan

The second step is to create your mentoring plan by aligning goals to the different mentoring skills. Create a document with three columns. In the first column, list the areas you wish to improve on for each mentoring skill. These areas will emerge from your self-assessment results. Then, in the second column, enter the strategies you intend to use to address each problem. Finally, use the third column to pose questions that will enable you to realize your development goals.

Select each of the three columns of the sample mentoring plan to learn more about the kind of information you should include in each.

Areas to focus on

For each mentor skill, enter the results of your self-assessments by articulating specifically what you've identified as areas to focus on. This makes your plan sharper and helps you focus on improving specific skills.

Strategies to address the problem

In the second column, you then enter practical strategies for how you intend to achieve your goals.

Guiding questions

To help you really reflect on how you're going to implement your strategies, add questions to the final column to guide your thinking. For example, ask yourself "What is the time frame in which I want to achieve this?" You should add relevant, guiding questions to this column for each of the six mentor skills in your plan.

Consider the example of Alan, the mentor. He considers the skill of "Listening and asking questions." He identifies from his self-assessment results that he needs to focus on listening to mentees more actively.

Alan then moves to the column of "Strategies to address the problem." Alan enters the strategies of "Practice active listening in all workplace situations," "Take notes of mentee achievements and concerns in every meeting," and "Review how to phrase open-ended questions."

Then he asks himself some guiding questions about how he can ensure he follows through on his strategies. He writes in the "Guiding questions" column: "What kind of improvements do I expect to see in one month, three months, and one year?" and "Who could I ask to help me achieve this?"

Question

Which statement best describes the process of creating a mentoring plan?

Options:

1. Once you've identified your goals and expectations, you should create a mentoring plan including areas to focus on, ways to make improvements, and guiding questions
2. The first column in your plan, "Areas to focus on," is the same as identifying goals and expectations

Answer

Option 1: This is the correct option. The second step of analyzing self-assessment results is to create your own mentoring plan for improvement. This plan will include specific areas to focus on, what to do about them, and guiding questions.

Option 2: *This option is incorrect. The first step of analyzing assessment results is to identify which of the six mentor skills you need to work on in order to meet your goals. "Areas to focus on" involves specific areas of these skills that need to change in order to meet those goals.*

Improving through action

The final and most important step to developing your mentoring plan is to bring about improvement through action. The key to this stage is focusing your thinking by asking yourself pointed questions about your plan and more general questions about your mentoring style.

Mentors can ask themselves a range of questions to help them reflect on their skills and record them in a journal. For example, they could ask some questions specific to their plan and goals such as "Why do I have a tendency not to prioritize my meetings with mentees?"

Or they can be more general questions about overall mentoring style. For example, a mentor might ask "Do I exemplify a pleasant manner and professional behavior with my mentees?"

Remember Alan, the mentor? He wants to improve his listening skills by listening actively to his mentees, taking notes, and phrasing questions the right way. To activate his plan and improve through action he asks himself "Am I clear in the way I ask questions and am I getting comprehensive answers?" This type of question is specifically related to one of the areas he wishes to focus on.

He also asks more general questions about his commitment to improve his mentoring style over time. He reflects "Do I use appropriate, nonjudgmental language in my discussions with my mentee?" and "Do I model the type of behavior and culture promoted by our organization in my conversations with my mentee?"

Question

Frank has been a mentor to Julie for one year. He is looking to improve his ongoing mentoring relationship with Julie and has completed a mentor self-assessment to assess his skills. His results indicate that he needs to improve in the areas of providing feedback and conflict resolution.

Which statements represent examples of the steps Frank should take when using his self- assessment results to improve his mentoring skills?

Options:

1. Frank sets "giving timely feedback specific to Julie's needs" as a goal for himself
2. Frank develops a strategy that will enable him to be more patient during conflicts and notes it in his plan for improving his skills
3. Frank asks himself specific questions about how he can make his feedback more timely and effective for Julie
4. Frank asks Julie to write a detailed report on how he deals with conflicts and says he'll add his own comments to the report later
5. Frank decides to be less critical of himself when assessing his feedback skills because he thinks Julie seems to understand his suggestions

Answer

Option 1: This option is correct. Frank uses his self-assessment results to set goals and expectations by identifying areas he needs to focus on in relation to mentoring skills.

Option 2: This option is correct. Using his results, Frank creates a plan by listing areas he
wants to focus on, strategies for addressing those areas, and questions to ask himself as he sets out to implement his improvement plan.

Option 3: This option is correct. To bring about improvement through action, Frank asks himself questions that are both specific to his goals and apply to his mentoring style in general.

Option 4: This option is incorrect. The purpose of learning and de-

veloping through self-assessment is that you identify your strengths and weaknesses yourself and develop a meaningful plan for improvement based on this.

Option 5: *This option is incorrect. The only way to achieve real, meaningful improvement is to be honest with yourself about both your strengths and weaknesses, work on them, and model a spirit of continuous development.*

Summary

Before you can assess yourself as a mentor, you need to understand the skills required to be a successful mentor. There are six skills that effective mentors often share: listening and asking questions; giving meaningful feedback; setting goals and expectations; building relationships; problem solving and conflict resolution; and advocacy. You can create your own self-assessment using relevant questions to test each skill.

You can then analyze your self-assessment results to enhance your mentoring skills and relationships. There are three steps to using your results for this analysis: set goals and expectations for yourself, create a mentoring plan, and improve through action.

ASSESSING MENTORING PROGRAMS

Benefits of evaluating programs

In order to ensure your mentoring programs are effective, you need to evaluate them. Decision makers need specific feedback about what's working well, why it's working, and the difference it's making to the organization overall. They can then decide whether to continue the program.

Reflect

What do you think would be the benefits of evaluating a mentoring program?

You may have noted that evaluating mentoring programs helps to pinpoint areas that need to be improved. In addition to this, it helps to show what parts of the program are providing value for the time and money being invested.

Evaluating the program can also provide positive reinforcement to the mentors. It shows them where they're succeeding. It also helps to show mentees that their work has paid off. When participants can see the difference in their performance at various stages of the program, it motivates them to achieve more.

Continuously evaluating programs ensures that they maintain high standards. Without evaluation, program participants may become complacent and not see the point in continuing.

Evaluation planning and measurements

Evaluating something as vast and dynamic as a mentoring program might seem daunting at first. The data you gather from ongoing formative assessments will feed into your evaluation. Also, summative assessments gathered at important milestones in the program, or at the end, also help to indicate what's working well and what isn't.

When approaching the evaluation, it helps to focus on **why** you're evaluating the program and to sort information into three categories. First, you're interested in the success of the program's processes – what elements of the design worked and what didn't. Second you'll want to know how the program affected the people involved. Finally, you should analyze data to assess the short-term and long-term effects on the organization.

When measuring program process outcomes, you should revisit your intentions for establishing the mentoring program. Then you can measure how successful it was in achieving its intended objectives.

For example, if one of the program objectives was to ensure a more efficient work environment, you may have set a target of a 20% increase in project turnaround times after one year.

Then at the end of the year, you can measure whether the program achieved this target.

When analyzing how the program affected the people involved, the main areas to consider are participant experiences and perceptions of the program. Try to take these into account in both ongoing evaluations and in more formal evaluations.

The elements you use for this category of your evaluation could include mentor and mentee perceptions of the program, reported levels of motivation, or levels of job satisfaction among program participants.

For example, you might have set a target that 80% of mentees will feel more satisfied in their jobs as a result of the program. You'll then test how successful the program was in meeting this target after a period of time.

The last category to include on your evaluation of a program is the effects on the organization as a whole. Often these will only become evident after the program has been operational for a period of time. The organizational effects will generally be focused on more in summative evaluations.

Measurable outcomes for organizational effects might include hard, bottom-line metrics such as sales turnover, market share, or employee retention. They could also include effects on softer metrics such as workplace culture, project turnaround times, or numbers of promotions.

For example, you may have set an organizational target of increasing team efficiency by 25% as a result of enhanced relationship skills taught through the mentoring program. You can then measure how successful the program was in achieving this target at the end of the year.

A document is shown titled "Organizational outcomes" and written as a sub-point is "Target: Increase team efficiency by 25% by end of year"

Question

Which statements are true about planning to evaluate mentoring programs and measurements you can use?

Options:

1. When preparing to evaluate a program, it helps to focus on why you're evaluating the program and to sort information into three categories – program processes, people involved, and organizational effects

2. To identify measurable outcomes, you should look back at the program's original objectives

3. Once you've identified measurable outcomes, you can set specific targets and measure these against the original objective on an ongoing basis and at the end of a period of time

4. You can only measure hard, bottom-line metrics when assessing organizational effects in your evaluation

5. When measuring the experience and perceptions of

program participants, only mentors' opinions will be taken into account because they are more experienced than mentees

Answer

Option 1: *This option is correct. Sorting your data makes evaluating the program more manageable and easier to understand.*

Option 2: *This option is correct. You can set measurable outcomes using the program's original objectives and use data from summative and formative evaluations to test the outcomes.*

Option 3: *This option is correct. You can use the measurable outcomes you've identified from program objectives to set specific targets and then compare these to the data collected in your evaluation.*

Option 4: *This option is incorrect. Organizational effects is the third category in your evaluation and it includes both hard elements, such as turnover, and soft elements, such as workplace culture.*

Option 5: *This option is incorrect. The participants involved category of your evaluation should include the experiences and perceptions of all participants in the program.*

Gathering data

To arrive at a satisfactory and comprehensive evaluation, data should be gathered from participants, managers, and program developers. To make the analysis richer, you should try to use both quantitative and qualitative assessments. Quantitative data usually involves numerical or statistical data. Qualitative data provides more descriptive insights into an issue or area of analysis. It can be gathered from interviews or observations.

Whatever type of data you need, make sure you collect it regularly. You can use various methods to do so:

- Self-assessments such as the mentoring self-assessment can be given to mentors, mentees, and any others affected by the program – such as customers or mentee supervisors, for example. They should be tailored to suit each type of audience.

- You can interview participants of the program about their experience and perceptions. This can be done individually or in groups.

-    Comparing individuals' personal development plans to the results they actually achieved also offers insights for the program evaluation.

-    Another option is to ask participants to keep logs or diaries of their experiences. They should be willing to submit these for evaluation periodically.

-    Managers and supervisors are well placed to give feedback by directly observing mentees. They can do this by assessing the differences in their performance that they feel were brought about by the program.

-    You could choose to bring a cross-section of people involved in the program together for group discussions about their experiences of the program. This group may include mentors, mentees, and managers.

-    Finally, you can use solid, statistical data in your evaluations. An example of this type of data would include sales or turnover comparisons between one period and another during the course of the mentoring program.

Assessing people's reactions

Once you've considered which elements to include, you can then start structuring the evaluation process. There are four levels you should consider when evaluating the impact of the program fully. First, analyze the reactions of the people involved. Second, assess whether the desired learning has been achieved. Third, investigate whether that learning has transferred to new behavior in the workplace. And finally, try to identify how the program benefits the organization overall.

Mentoring is primarily about people and how they learn and evolve as a result of working with other people. With this in mind, the first of the four steps – analyzing reactions of people involved – may be the most important step.

Measuring how people feel can be difficult because of the subjective and intangible nature of the data.

However, interviews and questionnaires that probe people's

opinions can provide realistic and valuable indicators of how well the program is working. It's also critical that such evaluations are carried out during the program – or shortly after it ends – when people's reactions are fresh in their minds.

Consider this example of gauging people's reactions to a mentoring program. Daniel is a mentoring program coordinator. He's interviewing Bernadette, a mentee, about her experience of the program so far. Follow along to see how Daniel uncovers what worked and what didn't for Bernadette.

Daniel: So Bernadette, how have you found your experience of the program so far?

Daniel asks inquisitively

Bernadette: I think it's been great! I'll admit I was nervous about it at first. I thought it could have been explained a bit better to us.

Daniel: Really?

Daniel asks in a concerned tone.

Bernadette: Um, it just seemed to be thrown at us when we started. I know the idea is to help us settle in but I didn't understand how intense it was going to be or how often I'd have to meet with my mentor.

Daniel: Yeah, that must have been a bit unsettling as a new employee! Do you think explaining the process in detail at the start would've helped you adjust better or would it have scared you more?

Daniel says in agreement

Bernadette: I guess explaining it a little better would have helped. But you're right, you don't want to scare people with too much detail either.

Daniel: How do you mean?

Bernadette: Well, I found other parts of the program really helpful and that was mainly because I was learning as I went along. Like the times I went along with my mentor to her client meetings... It felt really natural to learn the job that way. *Bernadette says in an upbeat tone*

Daniel asks simple questions and uses the answers he receives to probe deeper. This shows Bernadette that her opinions are valued and he's gleaning useful information.

Through Bernadette's feedback, Daniel learned the pros and cons of providing mentees with only a bit of information about the program before it begins.

Now that Daniel has learned the pros and cons, he can tweak how much information mentees are provided with at the start of the program. He can also decide which elements should be left for later on.

Question

A program coordinator is preparing an evaluation of a mentoring program.

Which actions are effective for assessing people's reactions?

Options:

1. Ask simple, direct questions
2. Gather feedback from participants
3. Get people's reactions during the program – or shortly after it ends 4. Focus more on quantitative data when assessing reactions
5. Consider the elements to include in the evaluation

Answer

Option 1: *This option is correct. Asking questions shows that mentees' opinions are valued.* **Option 2:** *This option is correct. Before you can proceed with analyzing other elements of the*
program you first need to find out what people thought of it.

Option 3: *This option is correct. In order to get the most valuable and accurate feedback, people's perceptions need to be fresh in their minds when you evaluate them.*

Option 4: *This option is incorrect. People's perceptions can be difficult to measure, so focusing on qualitative data gathered through interviews and questionnaires can add depth to the evaluation.*

Option 5: *This option is incorrect. You need to plan the evaluation first and then assess certain aspects of people's reactions.*

Assessing learning and behavior changes

As is the case with analyzing people's reactions, the second level – assessing whether learning has been achieved – may also prove difficult.

Because mentoring often teaches abstract skills, it can be difficult to evaluate changes in learning levels. For instance, if one of the program's objectives is to help new employees adapt to the organization's culture, it could be difficult to quantify whether this has occurred, and to what extent, after the program ends.

What you can do is focus on the objectives of the program and ensure to link assessments to these. So in the example of helping employees understand the organizational culture, you could carry out pre- program and post-program role-plays, interviews, or questionnaires. This will help to ascertain in a realistic way any improvement in a mentee's understanding of the culture and how things are done in the company.

Different types of testing techniques lend themselves to the assessment of knowledge, skills, or attitude change in mentoring programs. When specific knowledge change can be defined in a program's objectives, you can use techniques such as pre-program and post-program interviews, exams, and questionnaires to test for change. The results of these techniques can be easily compared among mentees and it helps you to assess how each mentee has improved in specific areas.

To assess whether mentees have acquired specific skills, you can observe them as they carry out tasks, perform simulated pre-program and post-program role-plays, and conduct case studies. These techniques help you assess how mentees perform when faced with a specific task as well as gauge how well they've improved their skill levels in specific areas.

Measuring changes in attitude is more challenging than measuring changes in knowledge and skill levels. Attitudes are difficult to gauge due to their subjective nature. You can, however, compare surveys, questionnaires, and mentor or supervisor observations given at the beginning of the program to those gathered at subsequent stages. Also, appropriate psychological assessments can help to monitor changes in attitude over time in relation to specific areas.

Consider the example of Anne, a mentee working in the HR Department of a large firm. Select each area involved in the assessment of desired learning levels to discover examples of how each type might be assessed.

Knowledge change

Anne is interviewed about her knowledge regarding employment law at regular intervals throughout her mentoring experience. She may also have to complete an exam on the organization's HR policies and answer questions about them in an informal interview at the beginning, middle, or at the end of the mentoring program.

Skill change

One of Anne's specific skill objectives is to be able to prepare payroll runs by the end of her program. Six months into the program and at the end of the program, she's observed as she carries out this task, and she's scored on her performance. She also has an objective to improve her communication skills, so she engages in real-life scenario role-plays on dealing with angry employees professionally. Her progress is tracked throughout the program.

Attitude change

At the beginning of the mentoring program, Anne's attitudes regarding people management and emotional intelligence were measured through psychological profile tests and informal interviews. These techniques are administered again after six months and at the end of the program to track her attitude changes as a result of her mentoring experience.

The third level of your overall program evaluation is concerned with assessing whether learning has transferred to actual changes in behavior. This usually involves gathering the opinions and observations of those who work with the mentee, including line managers, supervisors, peers, direct reports, and clients. These are the people best placed to assess the mentee's behavior on a regular basis.

Hard measures such as sales performance, client acquisition, or number of times a particular task is carried out successfully can also be used to measure learning transfer and behavioral change.

You can gather evidence about whether learning has transferred to actual changes in behavior in a number of ways:

- An increase in performance appraisal results may indicate if a positive behavioral change brought about through learning has occurred.
- An increase in positive 360-degree reviews of the mentee completed by peers, those who report to the mentee, and managers of the mentee.
- An increase in the number of mentors who want to continue with the program can be seen as a positive affirmation of the improvement in mentee behavior.
- Finally, in appropriate situations, gleaning feedback from clients who deal with mentees can be an excellent way to pinpoint improvements in behavior. Positive client feedback can also indicate a positive transfer of learning.

Question

A program coordinator wants to move to the second and third steps of program evaluation, assessing learning and determining whether it has transferred to improved behavior.

Which actions are appropriate to take to do this?

Options:

1. Administer tests before and after a mentoring program to mentees to measure their knowledge in certain areas
2. Schedule 360-degree reviews and performance appraisals
3. Look at sales performance and client acquisition
4. Focus on getting quantitative data to measure learning precisely
5. Determine what you want to measure

Answer

Option 1: *This option is correct. Administering a test before and after a mentoring program to assess knowledge can indicate whether learning has taken place as a result of the program.*

Option 2: *This option is correct. To assess whether learning has transferred to actual changes in behavior, you can gather the opinions and observations of those who work with the mentee.*

Option 3: *This option is correct. Improved performance on the job, such as an increase in sales and client acquisition, may be an indication that learning has taken place as a result of the program.*

Option 4: *This option is incorrect. While hard measures can be used in these steps, the best proof of positive learning and behavior change comes from the opinions of those who work with the mentee.*

Option 5: *This option is incorrect. At this point, you should know what you want to measure. This action is part of evaluation planning.*

The final level you need to consider in your program evaluation is assessing the program's impact on the organization as a whole. The techniques you use for this level can sometimes be combined with those used for the previous level: observing new behavior. Results of all program participants' 360-degree reviews, interviews, and questionnaires can be gathered and assimilated. This helps you to arrive at conclusions about how behavior changes are impacting the organization's culture and its bottom line.

The primary focus at this level of the evaluation is on assessing whether the mentoring program has helped the organization achieve its business aims.

The ideal scenario for a program coordinator is to be able to create a cause-and-effect relationship between the program's results and the organization's strategic aims. This can be hard to do as many of the benefits provided by mentoring programs are nonquantifiable, subtle, and long-term.

Before outlining metrics you can use, it's useful to note that program coordinators and decision makers need to be careful in their evaluation of organizational benefits. Try not to attribute improvements to the program where other factors may have played a bigger part.

For example, the organization may have recently acquired new senior managers who are likely to have had more of an impact than the mentoring program on short-term, quantifiable increases such as turnover or profit.

Keeping this in mind, investigating changes in key metrics still forms an important part of program evaluation.

To discover organizational changes resulting from the program, look for things such as increased sales performance and increased efficiency in the completion of tasks. You could also search for improvements in organizational culture as seen in an increase in reports of job satisfaction and staff retention. Try to discover financial benefits also, such as an increase in revenue or areas where costs have been lowered through extra efforts made by mentees.

To create a comprehensive evaluation, you should try to gather data for all four levels. This means you analyze the reactions of people involved, assess whether learning has been achieved, observe whether learning has transferred to new behavior, and identify benefits to the organization.

Additionally, for it to be useful, it shouldn't be a static report with no calls to action. It should instead be complete with a set of recommendations and practical suggestions for improvement.

The evaluation needs to promote and enhance what's good about the program and eliminate extraneous elements that aren't achieving any benefits or are wasting time.

Question

A program coordinator is carrying out the final step of his evaluation, assessing the effects of the program on the organization. Which actions should he take?

Options:

1. Use results from the previous level to make conclusions

about how behavior changes are affecting the organization's culture

2. Examine sales performance and increased efficiency in the completion of tasks

3. Link any positive changes in the organization to the mentor program

4. Focus solely on financial measurements at this level Answer

Option 1: This option is correct. The techniques you use for this level can sometimes be combined with those used for the previous level: assessing behavior transfer. This helps you to arrive at conclusions about how behavior changes are impacting the organization's culture and its bottom line.

Option 2: This option is correct. You can use measurements like these to try to identify a cause-and-effect relationship between the program results and the organization's strategic aims.

Option 3: This option is incorrect. Program evaluators need to be careful not to attribute positive changes to the program that may have been caused by other factors, such as a new manager.

Option 4: This option is incorrect. The primary focus of mentoring is about people; however, programs can also contribute positive changes to the organization's bottom line.

Summary

The benefits of evaluating mentoring programs include finding out whether the time and money invested in such programs are really paying off.

When assessing a mentoring program, assess participant reactions to it, and then look at whether desired learning was achieved. It's also important to investigate whether learning has transferred to changed behavior on a day-to-day basis. Finally, try to assess the impact on the company by linking program results to the business aims of the organization.

ENDING MENTORING RELATIONSHIPS

Ending relationships

Successful mentoring programs use mentoring self-assessments and assessments of the program to promote continuous improvement. However, all mentoring relationships must end.

Ideally, relationships end because the participants have achieved all of their objectives. However, in some cases, you need to end the mentoring relationship prematurely. As a mentor, you must be honest with your mentee and act when the relationship isn't working. Sometimes, the relationship has to end simply because of a change of circumstances.

Reflect

Why do you think it might sometimes be necessary to prematurely dissolve a mentoring relationship?

You may have noted that a relationship might need to end because of personality conflicts between the participants. For example, the mentor and mentee may have different communication styles that make it difficult for them to create an effective bond. When this happens, it's best to seek alternative mentors for that mentee if possible.

A mentoring relationship may also end prematurely if the mentee is not adapting well to the tasks and objectives that have been set.

Also, if overdependency occurs, mentors may need to dissolve the relationship in the manner agreed on with the mentee at the outset.

During the course of mentoring relationships, program coordinators should monitor their progress. They may realize from formative assessments that a relationship isn't working.

Mentors should also be aware of the organization's processes or policy regarding how to handle these situations. They should explain all this clearly to the mentee at the outset.

The organization should also try to ensure that there are no repercussions for participants if they feel the relationship needs to be dissolved.

End points are often laid out in the organization's mentoring program. At the start of the relationship, you will have to set objectives with your mentee about what you want to achieve. You should also make clear that the relationship will have to end and that you both need to keep this in mind throughout the program. It's important for mentors to explain to mentees that the end will probably be when the objectives are met or when the mentee has passed a certain milestone.

You should also have agreed on the methods you'll use to assess whether these objectives have been met throughout the relationship.

As you approach the end, you and the mentee should both be assessing the mentee's progress as well as how close the mentee is to becoming fully independent. Having a definite end point can provide greater focus during the program and provide closure at the end of the program.

Question

Why is it important to set an end point for all mentoring relationships?

Options:

1. It gives mentees a focal point that motivates them to achieve their objectives
2. It provides a sense of closure to mentees so that they can feel more confident that they have learned what they needed and are moving on

3. If the relationship goes on too long it might cost the organization too much in resources
4. It means that mentors can escape from poor relationships when the time comes

Answer

Option 1: *This option is correct. Without an end point mentees wouldn't have a target to achieve the expectations and goals you've set together.*

Option 2: *This option is correct. By reaching the end point of a successful relationship, mentees feel they've achieved what they needed to move on to the next level.*

Option 3: *This option is incorrect. Because end points provide focus during the program, the organization doesn't risk wasting valuable resources.*

Option 4: *This option is incorrect. End points are essential for successful relationships. If a relationship isn't working, it should be dissolved right away.*

Planning an exit strategy

Having a well-planned exit strategy can make it easier to end a mentoring relationship. The strategy should outline when the relationship should end. It could end when the objectives have been achieved, when the circumstances have changed, or when the relationship isn't working.

See each possible reason for ending a mentoring relationship to learn more about it.

Objectives have been achieved

When a relationship has specific objectives built into the plan at the outset, the achievement of these objectives signals the end of the relationship.

For example, a mentee might have the objective of achieving a certain level of competence in a skill or knowledge area. Once this has been achieved and measured, such as through an exam, the relationship ends.

Circumstances have changed

Sometimes a relationship may have objectives that are more general, abstract, or difficult to quantify.

For example, the intention may be simply to provide a mentee with some guidance and support to aid general career development. In these cases, there should still be a target, perhaps a period of time. At the end of that period of time, the mentee may move on to another more measurable set of objectives within the relationship, or the relationship simply ends in a manner agreed upon at the start.

Relationship isn't working

There may be a need to dissolve the relationship prematurely if it's not achieving what it was meant to, or if the participants don't get along. If measurable objectives aren't agreed upon early on, it can be difficult to determine whether the relationship is achieving what was intended. This is why it's important to monitor the relationship over time.

Consider this example of Tony, a mentor, and Rachel, a mentee. It's the beginning of their mentoring relationship and they're discussing the ground rules and objectives. Follow along as they plan the desired exit strategy and agree upon criteria for dissolving the relationship if the need arises.

Tony: So Rachel, I'm really glad that we're going to be working together for the next while. I think it's important that we discuss what you want to achieve from the relationship. What are your thoughts?

Rachel: Well, you know from the assessment results that I need to work on my communication skills, especially for dealing with clients.

Tony: Yes, I have some ideas for that.

Rachel: Great. Then there's my marketing exam in May.

Tony: OK, good. I think you have enough time to sufficiently improve your communication skills and prepare for the exam. *Tony says in an encouraging tone.*

Rachel: I hope so!

Tony: Definitely. I think then we should aim for May as our end point in that case. I'm confident you'll achieve the objectives by then.

Rachel: Sounds good to me.

Tony: Now if for some reason the relationship isn't working for either of us, we need to be honest and take action. Do you agree? *Tony explains in a positive tone.*

Rachel: Sure, we don't want to keep doing something if it isn't working. What do you think we should do?

Tony: If either of us feels there's a problem that we can't fix, we'll agree to end the relationship amicably and I will certainly help to find you an alternative mentor. Are you comfortable with that?

Rachel: I think that's completely fair. *Rachel agrees positively.*

Tony indicated to Rachel that there needs to be definite objectives for the relationship. He encouraged her to establish her own goals.

Tony also made it clear that the relationship will have to end at some point. He and Rachel chose May as the end point, as Rachel would hopefully have passed her exam and sufficiently improved her communication skills by then.

Tony and Rachel also worked out what they will do to dissolve the relationship if either of them feels it's no longer working the way it should.

Question

Which statements represent appropriate ways to plan an exit from a mentoring relationship?

Options:

1. A mentor and mentee agree that the relationship will end after the mentee passes the professional accountancy exams

2. A mentor and mentee agree that if the relationship isn't working, they'll dissolve it immediately and try to find an alternative mentor

3. A mentor agrees with a mentee to provide him with general career development guidance for six months

4. A mentor agrees to coach a mentee until she feels

ready to work independently
5. A mentor decides to dissolve a relationship because he isn't sure whether the mentee has achieved the object- ives

Answer

Option 1: *This option is correct. The mentor and mentee agreed at the outset that the exams are the official objective and the passing of them will signify the end of the relationship.*

Option 2: *This option is correct. Dissolving a relationship may some- times be necessary and it's important to agree early on when this might be necessary and how it should be done.*

Option 3: *This option is correct. Sometimes the objectives for a re- lationship act as general guidelines for the relationship but an end point always needs to be agreed upon to effectively focus the relation- ship.*

Option 4: *This option is incorrect. Even if the objectives are general and hard to quantify, a definite end point for the relationship needs to be agreed upon to focus learning.*

Option 5: *This option is incorrect. If the relationship isn't working you can dissolve it but you should be sure why before you do so.*

The end meeting

When the mentoring relationship is ending, the mentor needs to meet with the mentee. As they are approaching the end point, both the mentor and mentee should be preparing for it. Both should be considering the original objectives of the rela- tionship and comparing them to the outcomes of the experi- ence. To professionally dissolve the relationship in any exit scenario, mentors and mentees should review four key areas in the end meeting.

First you should review the outcomes of the relationship in terms of knowledge, skills, and behaviors that the mentee has acquired. Second, discuss in an honest way what the relation- ship didn't deliver. Sometimes, there's an informal phase that follows the end of a mentoring relationship. If it applies, you should then talk about your expectations for this phase. Finally discuss any areas in which the mentee might benefit from further mentoring in the future from other suitable mentors.

See each of the four key areas you should discuss in the end meeting to learn more about it.

Review outcomes

It's important to summarize with the mentee what's been achieved from the relationship. Identify what outcomes have come from the experience in terms of increased knowledge, skills competence, or improved behaviors. Mentees should leave knowing the lessons they have learned and how they'll help them in the future.

What relationship didn't deliver

Try to be honest with each other about what the relationship didn't deliver. This may be an intended objective or simply something one or the other had hoped for but hadn't stated explicitly. Perhaps you can suggest a solution that can help the mentee with any unsatisfied expectations.

Informal phase expectations

Some mentors may decide to offer informal support after the relationship ends officially. This depends entirely on what the mentor and mentee want and the policies of the organization. While you should stress that the mentoring relationship is over, you can still continue to offer occasional support for issues that were covered during the relationship. You need to discuss this phase with your mentee.

Further mentoring

The mentee may still have some areas that could be improved with further mentoring. You should discuss this with the mentee and offer suggestions for suitable mentors if relevant. A good mentoring relationship ends with both parties seeing the other as a positive and reliable
person to keep in their professional network.

Returning to the example of Tony and Rachel, they are now at the end of their mentoring relationship. Follow along as they review the outcomes before the ending.

Tony: So Rachel, we've finally reached the end. It's been quite a journey, hasn't it? Congratulations on your exam results!

Tony says in an upbeat tone.

Rachel: Thanks! I can't believe a year has gone by so fast. It's been a huge learning curve.

Rachel says in a happy tone.

Tony: Yes. We had some ups and downs but you got there. How do you feel about the experience? Did you get what you wanted from it?

Rachel: I think so. Our objective was to improve my communication skills. I've acquired two new client accounts all on my own.

Tony: Yes, that's great. And our other objective was the exam and that's checked off the list too!

Rachel: Yes it is! I have a lot more work to do though. That meeting with the client two months ago. I lost my composure a bit.

Rachel says in a serious tone.

Tony: That was a slight setback. Don't worry. I know some excellent mentors who could help you develop your communication skills further. And I'm always here to talk over a coffee if you need to.

Tony says in a slightly serious but genuine tone.

Rachel: Thank you very much, Tony. *Rachel says in an appreciative tone.*

Tony discussed with Rachel how she felt about the outcomes of their mentoring relationship. Because Rachel passed her exams and improved her communication skills, she and Tony are both happy they have achieved their objectives.

Rachel also brings up something she felt didn't go too well for her with regard to her objective of communicating more effectively with clients. Tony reassures her that it was only a setback. Finally, Tony informs Rachel that he'd like to continue a more informal relationship and offers to give her support if she needs it. He also offers to put her in touch with appropriate mentors for further mentoring.

Case Study: Question 1 of 2

Scenario

For your convenience, the case study is repeated with each question.
Nigel is a mentor to Harry at a consulting firm. Nigel has been mentoring Harry for general career development. Six months into the relationship, Nigel is frustrated that Harry doesn't seem to be progressing as he'd hoped. He finds it difficult to get along with Harry and Harry doesn't seem to take in any of the advice or complete any of the tasks Nigel has set.

Determine whether ending the mentoring relationship is carried out correctly by answering the questions in any order. When finished select **Next Page** to continue.

Question

At the outset of the relationship, it was agreed that their objective was simply to improve Harry's knowledge and skills and that they'd meet for as long as was needed. Both parties also discussed at this point that if the relationship isn't working they would take immediate action, request to end the relationship, and find a suitable alternative mentor together.

What did Nigel do right when preparing his relationship exit strategy with Harry?

Options:

1. They agreed at the outset the objectives of their relationship and what they'd do if the relationship isn't working
2. Nigel left the end point open because Harry is just developing some knowledge and skills
3. Nigel set objectives for the relationship and left the end point for that relationship open

Answer

Option 1: *This is the correct option. It was important that Nigel discussed at the outset the objectives and what to do if the relationship wasn't working.*

Option 2: *This option is incorrect. Nigel correctly identifies objectives and what to do if the relationship isn't working. He also should* *set a definite end point to focus the relationship.*

Option 3: *This option is incorrect. Nigel failed to inform Harry that the relationship must end or set a target for when this would be.*

Case Study: Question 2 of 2

Scenario

For your convenience, the case study is repeated with each question.

Nigel is a mentor to Harry at a consulting firm. Nigel has been mentoring Harry for general career development. Six months into the relationship, Nigel is frustrated that Harry doesn't seem to be progressing as he'd hoped. He finds it difficult to get along with Harry and Harry doesn't seem to take in any of the advice or complete any of the tasks Nigel has set.

Determine whether ending the mentoring relationship is carried out correctly by answering the questions in any order. When finished select **Next Page** to continue.

Question

Nigel arranges to meet with Harry to inform him of his intention to dissolve the relationship. They both agree that it's not working and Nigel opens a discussion to review the outcomes, discuss what went wrong, and go through a list of possible alternative mentors for further mentoring. When the issue of an informal relationship after the end comes up, Nigel says he doesn't want Harry to contact him again.

Which statements describe how Nigel dissolved the relationship professionally?

Options:

1. Nigel opened up a discussion with Harry about what went wrong during their relationship
2. Nigel sticks to his agreement to find a suitable alternative mentor for Harry based on his needs for further mentoring
3. Nigel did what he could to try to part amicably with Harry despite the relationship ending prematurely
4. Nigel didn't bother reviewing the outcomes as the relationship was ending prematurely

Answer

Option 1: *This option is correct. To ensure Harry learned from the experience, it was important to debrief him about where things went wrong before they parted.*

Option 2: *This option is correct. Despite the fact that Nigel and Harry didn't get along, it was Nigel's duty to honor his agreement and find a suitable alternative mentor.*

Option 3: *This option is incorrect. Nigel didn't consider or discuss a possible informal relationship after the end, which didn't make the ending amicable.*

Option 4: *This option is incorrect. Nigel correctly reviewed the outcomes of their relationship, so that Harry would learn from the experience.*

Summary

All mentoring relationships must come to an end. To ensure that the mentee stays focused and motivated, mentors should discuss and agree on objectives and a definite end point with mentees at the beginning of their relationship.

It's important to plan a suitable exit strategy for the end of the relationship. It might end because all of its objectives have been achieved, because it has reached an agreed point in time, or because the relationship isn't working as intended for some reason.

Mentors should meet with mentees at the end to review successful outcomes, lessons learned for the future, and what didn't go well. Mentors might also discuss the possibility of maintaining an informal relationship after the end and areas the mentee might benefit from further mentoring in the future from other suitable mentors.

Printed in Great Britain
by Amazon